HACKNEY AT WAR

HACKNEY AT WAR

JENNIFER GOLDEN

IN ASSOCIATION WITH HACKNEY ARCHIVES

Author's Dedication

This book is dedicated to the men and women of Hackney who gave their lives in the war against fascism 1939–1945.

First published in 1995
This edition published in 2009
Reprinted 2013

The History Press
The Mill, Brimscombe Port
Stroud, Gloucestershire, GL5 2QG
www.thehistorypress.co.uk

British Library Cataloguing in Publication Data.
A catalogue record for this book is available from the British Library.

ISBN 978 0 7524 5371 2

Typesetting and origination by The History Press
Printed in Great Britain

Contents

Acknowledgements

In compiling this book, many hours were spent at the Hackney Archives Department, from where the bulk of the source material originated. My special thanks are therefore due to David Mander, the Borough Archivist, and his colleague Peter Foynes, who spent many hours looking through committee minutes of the period and staff. I am also indebted to David for having suggested that I tackle this project in the first place.

Thanks are also due to Kay Owen who supplied the information on the Rossendale ARP centre. My love and thanks are also due to Gary Morton, who encouraged me, acted as unofficial historian and who saw little of me during the months of preparation for this history.

Preface

This second edition remains substantially the same as the original edition of 1995, with only minor corrections. The only section to have been substantially revised is, 'Studying the Second World War in Hackney' (pp. 117–118 in the original edition). Names, addresses and telephone numbers of the organisations listed have been updated by current staff members at Hackney Archives, with the help of colleagues from Hackney Museum, London Metropolitan Archives, and Museum of London, along with some of the information about collections held in the organisations concerned. The section has also been updated with email and website addresses where relevant. The information in the section headed 'Buildings and memorials of the Second World War in Hackney' remains as it was in the first edition.

Chapter 1

The Legacy of the Thirties

On the morning of Sunday 3 September 1939 the British people were gathered around every wireless set in the land to hear the declaration of war against Germany. Prime Minister Neville Chamberlain had delivered an ultimatum to Germany at 9 a.m. The Germans gave no response. At 11 a.m. war was jointly declared on Germany by Britain, India and the Colonies.

The wait for the inevitable was over, the British people feeling both a sense of relief and at the same time great trepidation.

The years leading up to the Second World War provided the British with mixed fortunes. The early part of the decade was underpinned by the spectre of the Great Depression. Mass unemployment persisted as heavy industry, concentrated especially in the North of England, collapsed. Social consciences were stirred by a sense of insecurity and injustice. The resilience of the Jarrow marchers demonstrated the bitterness felt by sections of the population against a government who it was perceived cared little for the problems of unemployment and poverty. Against these problems, the thirties were marked by rambling, hiking, the birth of the Youth Hostels movement, holiday camps, radio and the cinema. Up to 20 million cinema tickets were sold every week.[1]

But while traditional industries declined, new industries supplanted them. The growth of a manufacturing industry and the emergence of large-scale factory production were especially concentrated on the new arterial roads being built around London. Job opportunities proliferated for the skilled and semi-skilled worker. These were accompanied by the growth of suburbia and the extension of the London Underground. The only tube station within the boundaries of Stoke Newington, Hackney and Shoreditch, Manor House, was opened in 1932 as part of the extension from Finsbury Park to Arnos Grove. Many local residents would have commuted to their new places of work or alternatively would have left the area completely, preferring to live on the new suburban housing estates adjacent to the countryside. Others would have travelled into the City and West End every day to work. Others would have found employment in the hundreds of businesses and shops throughout the locality, vigorously promoted by the local Chambers of Commerce. There were a few large factories in the area such as the Berger Paints factory in Homerton and the confectionery, plastics and chemical works out at Hackney Wick. Shoreditch had the greatest concentration of manufacturing business mainly dealing in furniture, shoes and clothing. The *Hackney Gazette* of 19 August 1938 reports the opening in Shoreditch of 'one of the most up to date clothing factories in London' where it was hoped to employ 1,500 workers. Shoreditch also had its own film studios, the Gainsborough, which survived until 1949.

Others found greater job security and better working conditions in the growing area of local government. For example, Shoreditch Borough Council decided in 1938 to pay all temporary employees for bank holidays that fell during periods of employment. However, in proposing payment Labour Councillor F. James stated that as men were taken on to suit the convenience of the council, all work was temporary – there was no such thing as regular employment.[2] This statement gives an indication of the vulnerability of the local labour market. Nonetheless, the increasing role of local government was a provider of many new white collar jobs and new town halls were built for the Metropolitan Boroughs of Hackney and Stoke Newington in the latter part of the decade.

Before the Second World War, local authorities had greater powers than they have in the late twentieth century. Many of the functions carried out today by government and increasingly by the private sector were the responsibility of the metropolitan boroughs. Shoreditch, for example, claimed to be the first district in England to utilise the heat generated by burning its refuse for electricity, hence the motto on the borough arms – 'More Light, More Power'.

Local authorities were required under Acts of Parliament to promote activities to improve the health of the nation. The three local Metropolitan boroughs were at the forefront of disease prevention in the 1930s and provided services which encompassed sanitation, overcrowding and slum clearance, improvement in diet, diphtheria prevention and the eradication of household pests. Publicity campaigns were mounted to educate the public, with many activities aimed at schoolchildren. Such campaigns had a positive effect with only five deaths in Hackney in 1938 being attributable to diphtheria.[3]

Hackney and Shoreditch in conjunction with the London County Council embarked upon a radical five year slum clearance programme from 1930 to 1935, informed by reports from the Medical Officer of Health. Cases for demolition were referred to public enquiries where the Property Owners' Protection Association, representing the landlords, vigorously opposed demolition.

Many new housing estates were opened across the three boroughs replacing many of the slum areas. Hackney's first estate under the five-year plan was Powell House opened in 1934. This was soon followed by other estates including the Kingsmead Estate and Homerton's Nisbet House. Such publicly funded house building programmes had the added advantage of putting some of the unemployed back to work. By the outbreak of war, the population of the twelve London County Council estates in Hackney was 10,481. In March 1938 the King and Queen visited Hillcot House on the new Stonebridge Estate, Haggerston. The Queen was said to have been especially impressed by the spacious balconies and the electric fires, the King with the low rents.[4]

But while many of the residents of the three boroughs survived the 1930s to no great personal disadvantage, many people continued to live in relative poverty and poor housing conditions. Poor health often accompanied poverty. The *Shoreditch Citizen* of January 1939 reported an outbreak of typhoid in Shoreditch. Although the source was never traced it was believed that the outbreak had been caused by a contaminated person handling food. There were twenty-eight cases in the borough resulting in four deaths.

Controversy over a report by the Shoreditch Housing Association in 1938 was played out in the local and national press. The *Evening News* of 19 August 1938 reported:

> Growing up in Shoreditch is a grim business for the average child ... overcrowding, lack of playing facilities, bad washing arrangements, no outdoor recreations and no holidays out of Shoreditch are the principal evils. A third of the homes under review have no indoor water supply and nearly 70 per cent have no facilities for baths at all. Nearly half have nothing but a kettle for heating water.

The Mayor of Shoreditch and officials of the Borough Council vigorously defended measures that had been undertaken such as housing programmes and the appointment of a municipal midwife who pursued an education policy of encouraging hospital rather than home births, thus helping to reduce the borough's high infant mortality rate to fifty-four per thousand births in 1937, reported as the lowest on record for the London boroughs. The decline in the population of Shoreditch from 122,000 to 82,000 over the previous forty-five year period was also cited as a positive indicator in the general improvement of the living conditions of the residents of Shoreditch.[5]

The people of Shoreditch, Hackney and Stoke Newington were avid fans of the cinema. New cinemas were opening, even up to the outbreak of war. A special supplement to the *North London Recorder*[6] was published to celebrate the opening of 'London's newest cinema, the magnificent new Odeon in Hackney Road E2 by Christopher Stone, famed radio star'. Exactly four months before the declaration of war the Dalston Odeon opened its doors accompanied by the band of the 1st Battalion, The Royal Scots. An opening ceremony included an appeal for local charities, including the Hackney Day Nursery, a fund which created recreational opportunities for the male unemployed.[7]

The thirties were also marked as a decade when people continued to develop an insatiable thirst for knowledge. The documentary film was born. *The Picture Post* was published in 1938. People read books in increasing numbers. The excellent public library service in the three Metropolitan boroughs were complemented by smaller private lending libraries such as the Billet Library in Upper Clapton Road. Novels, plays, social surveys were all read. *The New Statesman and Nation* continued to inform the thinking public. A series called 'The Intelligent Man's Guides' was much in demand amongst the left-thinking intelligentsia. The issues instructed on the events of the time from a philosophical and political viewpoint.

Crowds congregate in Downing Street following the declaration of war on 3 September 1939. (Imperial War Museum, HU 36164)

The main political parties had by the late thirties contemplated the idea of a managed economy with national economic plans, influenced by the works of Keynes. However, the government was not disposed towards a general increase in public expenditure in order to facilitate the end of the Depression, although some money was allocated towards pump priming the public and private house building industry which had by 1935 removed some of the unemployed from the dole queues. The economic upturn was slow, limited and confined nearly two million people to the ranks of the long-term unemployed.

Although unemployment dropped with rearmament, there remained in the year up to the outbreak of war some 1.8 million registered unemployed.[8] The thirties could aptly be described as the decade of Walter Greenwood's *Love on the Dole*.

One Woman's War – Dolly (Doris) Andreetti

I lived in Gorsuch Street until the outbreak of war. My maiden name was Hiscock but we didn't like that name and so used the name Escott. I had four brothers and one sister. Dad was a casual docker and mum would take in washing. You could say we were poor. Dad could not always get work and we often went without food. We shared our house with another family who had the upstairs. We had two rooms and a scullery downstairs. One of my brothers caught smallpox which spread to the White family upstairs. We all had to be fumigated at St. Leonards Hospital. Fortunately my brother recovered. Things got better when I left school in 1934. I was fourteen at the time.

At the outbreak of war we moved to Caesar Street off Cremer Street. I worked in a gas mask factory before the war, at Arthur Burton's in Bunhill Row. I machined the white stitching around the goggles. They had to be perfect. If you missed a stitch you had to throw the whole thing out and start again, I was seventeen when I worked there. I also worked at Briggs in Hyde Road. I machined army tents. They were huge and I got a pound for each one. My friends and I didn't know the war was on its way. We were too busy having a good time – drinking and dancing. We went to the pictures two or three times a week, to the Britannia in Hoxton Street, the Hoxton in Pitfield Street, the Dalston in Dalston Lane and the Savoy in Stoke Newington. We had our clothes made by a dressmaker. We used to buy material down Wentworth Street and would have costumes made. We always wore a hat, we used to buy them from Pimlico Walk, down Hoxton Street, and high heeled court shoes black suede with the toes cut out.

I met my husband Vic when I was seventeen at the Social Club in Pitfield Street. He was a professional boxer and his dad had a cafe down Hoxton Street at the time.

As I said, we didn't really know what was going on at the time but one Sunday morning, it must have been the day war was declared on Germany, the sirens went off. We were running around like lunatics. We had no shelters to go to. No one in Gorsuch Street knew where to go.

Vic and I got married in June 1940. He was in the Air Force by that time. I can remember one weekend in August when he was home on leave with his friend Jock. We were on our way to a pub in Hoxton Street when the bombs started falling. We just didn't know where to run. Trenches had been dug in the gardens of the Geffrye Museum and they took a direct hit. People were killed.

People decided to act for themselves and they cleared out the railway arches in Cremer Street despite the noise of the trains and the anti-aircraft gun. My mum, brothers and lots of people went there. People lived in the arches for most of the time during the Blitz. When the bombing got really bad I went to Wales for a while, to Haverfordwest where Vic was based, but I came home after a few months. I went down Old Street tube a couple of nights with my sister, Lit, but I didn't like it. It was too overcrowded and I didn't like the feeling of being under the ground.

I can remember that people were being moved out of Gorsuch Street into the new flats in Nuttall Street. Loads of people got killed down Nuttall Street. One family of thirteen were wiped out except for one sister. The wife of a friend was one of those killed. She was just a bit older than me.

I can also remember lots of people being killed from the cottages behind the Basing House pub next to Shoreditch Fire Station.

While Vic was away I worked as a machinist between the bombings. War work was compulsory if you were not married.

My father-in-law had been born in Italy and came to England when he was four years old, but because he had never taken out British citizenship he was classed as an enemy even though he had married an English girl and he had four sons fighting in the British armed forces, He was allowed no maps, no radio, no bicycle and he had to report to the police every week. He was made to do work under the direction of the security forces.

When my husband was away I lived with my mum in Caesar Street. I had the upstairs rooms. We had a cold tap in the house, but no hot water. We had an outside toilet in the yard.

London County Council flats in Nuttall Street after bombing on 29 September 1940. Thirteen people from one family and many others died in this incident.

My mum had been offered a flat in Nuttall Street. If she had accepted we could have been killed.

Despite everything, we always had a good time during the war. We were always down the pub singing and dancing and always going to parties at the weekends.

We didn't go without. There was a big black market operating, especially in tinned goods and American nylons which we all wanted because they never wore out. We never went short.

I remember taking my ration book to the butchers in Hoxton. If we gave him some extra money he would give us extra meat. There was a Welsh dairy down Cremer Street. The lady there would offer me butter and tins of salmon and other things that were difficult to get. If you were pregnant you could get bananas down Hoxton Market.

There was a lot of thieving going on, lots of goods for sale. People would come knocking at our doors asking whether we wanted to buy things.

When I was pregnant I was forcibly evacuated to Hitchin. I stayed at a cottage with a widow and her son. I nearly froze to death. She only burnt small blocks of wood on her fire. I suppose she had no money. One night I had to sleep in a fur coat. I was so cold I came home one weekend by bus from Luton. I remember having to go to hospital for a check up shortly before my son, Victor, was born. The doctors said I had high blood pressure and had to stay in hospital. I was so glad – I could be in a nice warm place. After the birth I had to come back to Caesar Street.

The bombing kept on until the end of the war. You never knew when it would start. They eventually got round to building shelters, concrete ones in the street for those people without gardens. I didn't use them. When the bombing got bad I would go down the arches at Cremer Street, though I tended to stay at home. One night my sister Lil and myself went down to the cinema in Hoxton. The red warning light came on the screen telling us that there was an air raid on. We left and I ran all the way back to Caesar Street with my nephew in my arms – I was that frightened. My mum was looking after Victor back at home on her own.

Sometimes you would see deserters from the forces in the pubs. They would often be followed by the police. Everyone could recognise the police. They would always be big and they wore the same style suits and macs. The deserters would go into the ladies' toilets and escape through the windows. I didn't know any of them personally. All my husband's friends did their national service and one of his brothers was killed in the air force in India.

When the end of the war came, there was a huge party down Caesar Street but we went for a knees up at the pub – Charlie Wright's down Pitfield Street. We moved to 29 Aske Street after the war. My sister and I gave a man a fiver each to get the house.

CHAPTER 2

The Political Scene

In Britain, the years up to the declaration of war were marked by the appeasement of Germany. The underlying causes of appeasement can arguably be identified by a number of considerations: the mass pacifist movement which had existed since the end of the First World War and had remained a potent force; Britain's lack of preparedness for war; pro-German sentiments expressed by ministers such as Lord Halifax and the inexperience in foreign affairs of Neville Chamberlain. The former Prime Minister, Stanley Baldwin, had gone as far in 1935 as saying that to arm Britain would have cost his government the mandate to continue to govern.[1]

Chamberlain became Prime Minister following the resignation of Baldwin, fifteen days after the Coronation of George VI. He had previously served as Minister of Health and Chancellor of the Exchequer. He had no direct experience of foreign policy matters. A.J.P. Taylor[2] has remarked that it was an act of fate that Chamberlain should become Prime Minister during a period when international affairs had assumed primary importance.

In 1938 Anthony Eden resigned as Foreign Secretary in protest at Chamberlain's inactive foreign policy leaving no active opposition within the Cabinet. In the autumn of 1938 Chamberlain's government resolved not to resist German attacks on Czechoslovakia. Instead, Chamberlain pursued negotiations with Hitler, in conjunction with France, for a gradual ceding of land by Czechoslovakia to the Germans, against the will of the Czech government. But Hitler's demands for Czech land intensified. Chamberlain appealed to Mussolini to convene a peace conference between Britain, France, Germany and Italy at which a negotiated settlement could be imposed upon Czechoslovakia. Chamberlain returned to London in the role of the man who had brought peace to Europe but having very little understanding that the demands of fascism were insatiable.

Not surprisingly, the Czech government sought to protect themselves against all external pressures and ordered general mobilisation. France in turn mobilised 600,000 troops. In autumn 1938 Europe stood at the brink of war. Chamberlain made a further trip to Munich and colluded in the forced annexation of the Sudetenland by Germany. The First Lord of the Admiralty, Duff Cooper, resigned in protest. The initial relief that Chamberlain had bought peace soon gave way to shame when German troops marched into Bohemia and Moravia in March 1939. The Chamberlain government was humiliated. The period of appeasement was at an end and Chamberlain was forced to concede that Western Europe was being sucked into war. Rearmament which had progressed slowly since 1935 became a pressing necessity.

The Spanish Civil War and the rise of fascism dominated international politics in the late 1930s:

> The controversy provided for the generation of the thirties the emotional experience of their lifetime. It has been rightly said that no foreign question since the French Revolution has so divided intelligent British opinion or, one may add, so excited it.[3]

The Spanish Civil War gave a practical opportunity to oppose fascism. British intellectuals on the political left largely supported the Spanish Republican movement under attack from German and Italian armed forces. Over 2,000 men from Britain fought alongside the Republicans. The majority were workers, in particular unemployed miners.[4]

The Spanish Civil War proved to be a catalyst for the left outside the Labour Party, in particular the Communist Party. Although only a few thousand in number, the Communist Party was an active promoter of Victor Gollancz's Left Book Club, which had acquired some 60,000 members during the period of the Spanish Civil War. Local readers groups were set up and the Labour Party was faced with the major problem of how to attract middle class support from groups like teachers who were more attracted by the texts offered by the Left Book Club than by Labour Party policy.[5]

Substantial support for the Spanish Republican cause had come not only from sections of the political left but also from the Church and other organisations in the form of funds and humanitarian aid. While the Western Powers of Britain and France agreed a policy of non-intervention in the war in Spain, substantial numbers of refugees were allowed into Britain. The *Hackney Gazette* reported on 400 Basque refugees being cared for by the Salvation Army at the Congress Hall in Linscott Road. Brigadier J. Martin who was in charge of the children said:

> The youngsters are not settling down too badly, but the girls are much better than the boys. The trouble is that these children have had no schooling since the war started and they are completely undisciplined. The boys go climbing together over the walls and roofs like little monkeys. For the most part they have no sense of religion, and no use for the Church. They seem to have Communist sentiments.[6]

Although the voters of Hackney, Stoke Newington and Shoreditch largely supported the Labour and Conservative Parties in elections to the council and parliament,

A British Union of Fascists rally held in Victoria Park in 1936.

Hackney and East End politics were imbued with opposing ideological perspectives not commonly found elsewhere with such vigour.

The Fascist movement led by Sir Oswald Mosley had capitalised upon the economic crisis and mass unemployment of the early 1930s. Mosley had set up branches in Hackney, Shoreditch and Bethnal Green and although anti-Semitic campaigns took place in all provincial cities with a substantial Jewish population, it was in the East End and in parts of Shoreditch and Hackney where the effects of violent Nazi inspired activity were perhaps most keenly felt.

While members of the local Labour and Liberal Parties spoke out against the rise of fascism, the Communist Party promoted political education and action against the fascist movement amongst the trade unions and tenants' organisations of the East End. Anti-fascist activity was at its most public at the Battle of Cable Street on 4 October 1936 and a march the following weekend through the centre of Mosley territory in Bethnal Green to a rally in Victoria Park.[7]

The success of Cable Street allowed the Communist Party to orchestrate a campaign which had its roots in Stepney against slum landlords. By 1939 rent strikes against both slum landlords and local councils had taken hold in a mass tenants' movement across England. Communist led rent strikes took place in Shoreditch ensuring that the local population was exposed to the two opposing political ideologies. The ongoing war in Spain brought these conflicts into sharper focus.

In 1937 William Joyce stood as a candidate for the LCC elections in Shoreditch. His election address to the voters was explicit in the British Union of Fascists' (the BUF) hatred of the Jewish community and the alleged power base of the Jewish establishment:

> Dear Fellow Citizens,
>
> We appeal as candidates of the British Union for your votes in the London County Council election on March 4th next. We are blackshirts who follow Mosley. We are pledged to fight to the end for the People's Cause against the tyranny of Jewish power. So we ask you by your votes to give the Parties of Jewry 'notice to quit'. You have now had experience of Conservative, Liberal and Labour rule in London. That experience has proved to you that they are all the same. . . . None of these Parties can help the people because they are the parties of Jewish Finance.[8]

Although the Labour candidate topped the poll with more than 11,000 votes, Joyce polled over 2,500 votes, an indication of the sizeable power base the British Union of Fascists had in Shoreditch at the time. In the months leading up to the outbreak of war, Joyce and his family escaped to Berlin from where he became famous as Lord Haw Haw for his radio broadcasts designed to undermine the British people. He was captured by the allies at the end of the war and was hanged in Wandsworth Prison in 1946.

In February 1939 the fascists broke up a meeting held at Shoreditch Town Hall to raise funds for the local Ambulance for Spain Committee. The speakers, Mr Ernest Thurtle, MP for Shoreditch, Professor J.B.S. Haldane and Mr Ernest Brown, of the Spanish Medical Aid Committee, were shouted at and the stewards appointed for the meeting were helpless in coping with the 200 fascists who commandeered the meeting. A smoke bomb and fireworks exploded in the hall and fighting spilled over into the street outside before the fascists marched to a rally in Hoxton Square singing 'It's a long way to Tipperary' as they went.[9]

The breaking up of meetings appeared to be a regular fascist tactic. The *Hackney Gazette*[10] also reports that a meeting held a few days later at Hackney Town Hall, addressed by Mr Fred Watkins, Member of Parliament for Central Hackney, was also disrupted by heckles and fascist songs with the chorus 'You can't beat the boys of the BUF that made old England's name'.

In his reminiscences, entitled *The 43 Group*, Morris Beckman recalls:

> During the Thirties I was a pupil at Hackney Downs Secondary School, in the heartland of the pre-war activities of the BUF. Their intimidatory violence turned a pleasant enough life into one of apprehensive misery. Jewish people were afraid to venture out after dark and even during the day, gangs of arrogant Blackshirts roamed the street abusing and molesting Jews they encountered. It was also unpleasant for non-Jews but they, at least, were not the direct target of

The windows of Jewish-owned shops were smashed following a meeting of the British Union of Fascists in Victoria Park in 1936.

> abuse and violence. I remember going out at night and keeping a wary watch for Mosley's gangs. Fortunately they tended to be noisy, and one could hear the chants of 'Heil Mosley!' and 'Get rid of the Yids!' in time to dive down a side street or into a front garden thick with bushes. War put an end to all of that.[11]

Albert Cullington who served as one of Hackney's mayors during the war recalled the activities of Mosley and his followers in Hackney:

> During the years prior to the outbreak of World War II, the Fascist movement of this country was particularly strong in Hackney. There were constant Fascist meetings held on street corners with particular attention being paid to Ridley Road. The Fascists rented premises at Balls Pond Road, Dalston, at Elsdale Street in South Hackney and at premises near Homerton railway station. Feeling against them was very strong particularly from the Jewish community. The Fascists had also held meetings at the Kings Hall which was owned by the Borough Council. Strong pressure was being put on the Council, of which I was a member, to refuse lettings to the Fascists. We were advised by the then Town Clerk that we should require strong reasons for refusing Fascists meetings as they were ratepayers in

respect of three separate premises and as such had the same rights as other rate-payers and we might be open to legal action with possible damages being awarded against us. After a great deal of thought and discussion, it was decided to grant the current application and employ a shorthand writer to take a report, the contents of which proving Jew-baiting and racialism, would constitute adequate grounds for refusing subsequent applications i.e. action likely to cause a breach of the peace. Subsequently the Town Clerk reported to us that the cost of the shorthand report would exceed the amount of rent from the letting and he advised that the District Auditor might surcharge the committee the amount involved. Finally as a way out, I was asked whether I would do the report as I was a shorthand writer. A press ticket was specially printed for me and on the night of the meeting I duly sat at the press table. The Fascist rally took place at the Kings Hall on December 2nd 1936. By 7.30pm there were about 100 ticket holders inside, queues were being formed outside, scores of Fascists were present in uniform. By 7.50 the hall was practically full. There was no chairman of the meeting, the speaker a Mr Joyce, just walked onto the platform, gave the Fascist salute and started right away.[12]

The Jewish community in the areas of Stoke Newington, Shoreditch and Hackney had mixed perceptions on the political causes of the war, although they were united in their abhorrence of the Nazi persecution of Jewish people.

They campaigned unceasingly through the Workers' Circle and other organisations to publicise the attacks upon the Jewish people on mainland Europe and to raise funds. Pre-war correspondence describes: 'the beating up of people; the attack on students; the introduction of Ghetto benches in the universities, the economic boycott to which the Fascist or semi Fascist governments are showing a blind eye; the call for the strongest protests on the part of humanity.'[13]

The Workers' Circle Friendly Society, an organisation based in the East End but drawing on members throughout the Hackney, Shoreditch and Stoke Newington areas, had been formed in 1908. Membership was made up of Jewish trade unionists who chose not to join other Jewish organisations because of their religious and class bias. There was something of a stir when 'Branch number 9' circulated the following resolution:

In view of the fact:

1) that the present war between Britain and France on one side and Germany on the other is being fought for a new redivision of colonies, markets, spheres of influence and sources of raw materials, i.e. that it is an imperialist war;

2) that the sufferers in such wars are always the masses of the people whose blood will be shed; whose standards of living are being attacked and reduced; whose democratic rights are being continually limited;

3) that for the Jews in particular, this war holds special dangers; as the effects of the war become more obvious, as suffering and want increase; as the

> discontent grows, the need to divert all this becomes more necessary – and the policy of the scapegoat is resorted to;
>
> This quarterly meeting of Branch number 9 of the Workers' Circle, held on 24 December 1939 resolves:-
>
> a) that the above be made clear to the mass of the people in general and the Jews in particular;
>
> b) that it is the task of branches of the Workers' Circle as the leading Jewish Workers' organisation to use their efforts to make the above understood;
>
> c) that this resolution be circulated to Workers' Circle Branches and the press.[14]

Correspondence followed between branches of the Workers' Circle for months afterwards, either supportive of the resolution of Branch number 9 or outwardly hostile towards it.

In the early part of the war, the government gave serious consideration to the problem of 'Fifth Columnists' – those of the population who were subverting the war effort at home. The Home Secretary, Sir John Anderson, in a House of Commons speech, said:

> A certain body known for its anti-Semitic and Nazi propaganda has instructed its members to become rumour-mongers and channels for verbal Nazi propaganda. Measures considered to be necessary for the safety of the civilian population are to be made fun of. For example, parents who evacuated their children to safe areas must be made to think that evacuation was unnecessary. The object here is to get people to bring back their children to London and thus defeat measures taken in their interest. This is the way these people operate.[15]

This reference was to the BUF, many of whom were conscripted into the armed forces, interned or went underground from where they continued to produce leaflets for distribution to the public. Morris Beckman recalls how despite internment, much of the BUF political machine was able to be revived at the end of the war:

> The police confiscated many records belonging to the fascists at the outbreak of war, but they left much in Mosleyite hands. Valuable records, including names and addresses, files and account books were taken to a bomb-proof hide out in a railway arch warehouse bordering Hackney Downs. They lay under the Liverpool Street to Enfield railway line until recovered by the fascists after the war.[16]

Against this background of political turmoil and international uncertainty, preparations were made for the protection of the civilian population in the event of war.

CHAPTER 3

The Organisation of Civil Defence

The initial impetus for the development of Air Raid Precautions (ARP) had come from the Home Office as early as July 1935. In a circular sent to all London local authorities, the Home Office outlined the various services needed for the protection of the public in the event of air attack and proposed a conference of all interested parties for October of that year. Hackney, Shoreditch and Stoke Newington Borough Councils all sent representatives.

The emphasis was very much on protection against gas attack from the air and decontamination should that occur. For the general public the advice was to be 'that everyone who can, should stay indoors in a gas proof room or refuge'. Each local authority was 'to make such plans as may be possible whereby . . . shelters could be made gasproof and given perhaps protection against blast and splinters of high explosive bombs'. Only those required for emergency service were to be provided with respirators. The widespread distribution of gas masks was not envisaged.[1]

Responsibility for the organising of plans and preparations for different aspects of ARP was to be divided among the authorities 'in accordance with their peace time allocation'. Councils were asked to consider how 'existing organisation could be adapted, in time of emergency, to carry out ... work which would be required to help to save and preserve life and to keep essential services in operation'.

The reaction of the local authorities to the Home Office initiative differed. Shoreditch Council, perhaps reflecting the pacifist views of its Member of Parliament, Ernest Thurtle, and the deputy Mayor during this period, Dorothy Thurtle, daughter of George Lansbury, rejected the concept of ARP and resolved:

> That so far as this Council is concerned we recognise our responsibilities for the services under our control and will, of course, continue to maintain them adequately in all circumstances in the interests of our population. We can, however, be no party to misleading the people into a false sense of security.[2]

Hackney and Stoke Newington Councils began to develop ARP contingency plans in line with the Home Office recommendations despite, in the case of Stoke Newington, being petitioned by local bodies to support the position adopted by Shoreditch. The following letter was received by the Stoke Newington General Purposes Committee from the National Amalgamated Union of Shop Assistants and Warehousemen and Clerks:

> The Branch representing the shop assistants of the Borough calls upon the council to refuse to operate the Government's Circular on Gas Raid and Air Raid precautions and draws attention to the following observation: Such precautions must be real. The measures proposed by the present government are more in the nature of a cruel and sinister hoax on the population. This has been made only too plain by those who have a knowledge of what the danger from the skies implies. Gas masks are no protection, because of such murderous gases such as 'Mustard' and 'Lewisite' which attack the whole body . . . [3]

The same committee also received a resolution from the London Co-Operative Society urging 'the Borough Council not to institute any form of Air Raid drill as it would give a false sense of security whilst creating the very mentality which leads to war'.[4]

By June 1936 Hackney had prepared an 'extremely well thought out' ARP draft scheme. Hackney was the first council in the county to do so[5] and remained pre-eminent in ARP work up to and after the outbreak of war. By January 1937 the council had appointed a full-time ARP Officer. ARP booklets were distributed,[6] lectures for council staff arranged and a film produced following a Ministry of Housing report on anti-gas precautions. The film was never publicly screened because the portrayal of the effects of gas attack was considered too appalling.

By January 1938 a full ARP scheme had been prepared detailing decontamination centres, areas to be evacuated, transport, communications and the responsibilities of the warning, rescue and repair functions of the ARP service.[7] In May 1938 the London County Council, which was responsible for schools, agreed upon a policy of closure of all its schools should air attacks become likely. Training of school keepers began later that year. In February 1938 Hackney put out a call for 2,500 volunteers to serve as air raid wardens. Women as well as men were eligible. By September 1,635 volunteers had come forward and every house in the borough had been canvassed to establish the likely need for gas masks.

In 1937 the government had passed the Air Raid Precautions Act and the Civil Defence Act followed in 1939 ending the period of voluntary local authority initiatives towards ARP work. Both Acts conferred duties upon local authorities and the public utilities. The Civil Defence Act enforced local authorities to provide government with a report stating: what measures they had taken or were taking to provide air raid shelters for their employees and the public; that a suitable proportion of those employees had been equipped to give first-aid treatment to deal with the effects of gas, and to fight fires; and what measures had been taken or would be taken to secure the functioning of their responsibility in the event of hostile attack.

By July 1938 the ARP programme in Hackney had entered a new phase with the acquisition and adaptation of the former employment exchange at 219-31 Mare Street as a permanent headquarters for the ARP service. The *Hackney Gazette* described the building in its report of the opening ceremony:

> The ground floor hall contains 28,000 civilian gas masks, stored in steel racking, for distribution to the public in time of emergency. Training classes will be held in this hall to enable volunteer assemblers to become conversant with their duties. In the first floor hall is arranged a permanent exhibition with a refuge room, scale models of shelters and illustrating the adaptation of existing basements, apparatus showing the working of the respirator and exhibits of all types to assist volunteers in training.
>
> At the rear of the building different types of road surfacing such as tar-macadam, stone sets, cement and wood paving, have been laid in order that decontamination squads may receive practical training. Three hundred of the Council's employees have volunteered for this part of the work and 240 have nearly completed the course . . . at the conclusion of his inspection of the headquarters Wing-Commander Hodsoll informed the Mayor and the Town Clerk (Dr. Tee) that it was the finest and best-equipped headquarters of any that he had seen in the whole of the country.[8]

The Northern Report Centre for ARP work in Hackney was also opened in 1938 at 24 Rossendale Street, Clapton. The building has survived virtually intact and was listed in 1993 by The Department of National Heritage, who described the building as follows:

> Bunker built as Air Raid Precaution Centre. 1938. Concrete, approximately 2 metres thick and set about 1.2 metres below ground level as a half basement. Crudely built walls with shuttering lines; some shrapnel damage, particularly to the west face. Rectangular in plan, with long axis running on east-west line; all corners chamfered except for the southwest. Steps down at south corner, west face, into air lock: pair of steel doors with portholes, rubber gaskets and furniture of original design. Corridor along south wall giving access to Messenger's Room, Telephone Room and, at the east end of the bunker, the Supervisor's Office and Map Room is a circular escape hatch to air lock; outer lock door has been removed. Entered off Messenger's room, and located at the west end of the block, are the Store Room and Machine Room. The Machine Room retains original plant for air supply and purification and emergency electricity supply, as well as ventilator ducts running from this room to the rest, along the north wall. The Electric generator pedal driven by a twin bicycle frame survives as does the tiered air filter units made by Sutcliffe Speakman and Co., Ltd. of Leigh, Lancs. On the north wall is a battery control unit made by the Chloride

The Mayor of Hackney, Councillor Wayman, and other dignitaries taking part in civil defence training.

Electrical Storage Co. Ltd., linked to a chest on the floor which held a 12 volt battery for emergency lighting and heating. Two 12 volt light fittings survive in the ceiling. The storey above, flat roofed and made from brick, has been extensively altered: the earliest section is to the south. Concrete roof with shuttering lines throughout upper floor. The Rossendale ARPC was the northern report centre, part of a system which included a main centre located below Hackney Town Hall. It was used to co-ordinate information on bombing raids, for the deployment of teams for emergency rescue and repair work.[9]

In June 1938 Hackney's ARP Committee organised an exhibition on the gas proofing of buildings. Alderman Herbert W. Butler, the Committee Chairman, put the views of the committee:

. . . Opinions might have differed some time ago, but to-day every public authority agrees that, in the view of certain events throughout the world, any authority which refused to believe that the citizens of this country should be organised for the protection of themselves would be swept out of office and would deserve such a fate. Local authorities had a bounden duty to take all the necessary precautions against 'this horrible thing'.[10]

Inside the Lebon's Corner ARP shelter in May 1939. The cramped steel construction measured only 12 feet by 7 feet by 7 feet.

ARP initiatives had also been pursued in Stoke Newington despite the earlier political protests. An ARP committee had been established in December 1935, following the Home Office Conference. Lectures and courses for the public and council staff were organised, but it was not until January 1938 following the 1937 Air Raid Precautions Act that a comprehensive scheme was considered. In March 1938 the Assembly Hall was packed to overflowing to hear Captain A.J. Toyne, of the Home Office ARP Department, and others asking for 2,000 volunteers. Some 263 people volunteered immediately. To increase recruitment three head wardens were appointed to canvass throughout the borough. In addition, a 'school of instruction' was to be opened which would give the necessary training. The borough could provide large public shelters for people caught on the streets during air raids and help to provide gas proof rooms in individual houses. Other work would entail the organisation of rescue and first-aid parties, casualty stations, base hospitals and decontamination squads. Under such a scheme, the borough required one air raid warden to every 500 members of the population.[11] The Stoke Newington training school opened in June 1938 and according to the *Daily Telegraph*:

> training will be carried out under the auspices of the British Red Cross Society and demonstrations will comprise the bursting of persistent gas bombs on windows before treatment with cellophane and after, the preparation of a refuge room and similar experiments. Several nuns from convents will attend the course.[12]

In Shoreditch the initial reluctance of the council to become involved in ARP work abated due to a combination of the deterioration of the international situation and the passing of the Air Raid Precautions Act. An ARP Officer was appointed in April 1938 and council staff were sent for training in anti-gas measures.

The *Hackney Gazette* reported the deliberations of the Shoreditch ARP Committee in July 1938. The chairman of the committee is reported as having said that on grounds of cost, the council had earlier declined to do anything until such time as the government came to their rescue. But the *Gazette* pursued a critical approach by suggesting that council opposition had been based on the belief that the proposed precautions would be futile and would have the effect of making the people more war-minded. However, against the growing crisis in Europe the committee had finally decided to propose the storage of 30,000 respirators in the basement of the Town Hall.[13]

The 'national crisis week' in September 1938 galvanised Shoreditch into action. At the height of the Munich crisis five first-aid posts were established at Curtain Road, Crondall Street School, Napier Street School, the Model Welfare Centre in Kingsland Road and at the Haggerston Baths. Some 160 premises were requisitioned for providing emergency air raid shelter and 160,000 sandbags were distributed. The digging of trenches was started in Geffrye Gardens and Aske Gardens. Boy Scouts had volunteered as messengers and over 1,000 people had volunteered for ARP work. Captain Charles Hollis, the Shoreditch ARP Officer, told *The Star*:

> We are using lantern slides of ARP work at local cinemas, gramophone records of borough officials explaining various phases of the work and covering the Borough with posters.[14]

By the end of the month and under government instruction, the distribution of 90,000 gas masks had commenced and Captain Hollis told the *Gazette*:

> At least nine-tenths of the population have been measured already, and there will be facilities for those who have not been fitted to have this done and get their respirators at the same time. . . . Shoreditch has shown that it has the right spirit in this time of crisis. We have sent out S.O.S.'s for helpers and they have been coming along in their hundreds to us as late as 9 and 10 o'clock at night to work as gas mask fitters, clerks, messengers and so on.[15]

Interviewed by the *Hackney Gazette* the following October Councillor T.J. Sillitoe stated:

> The residents of Shoreditch came forward in their hundreds to help us out of our difficulty, and the business houses of Shoreditch did all they could for us. Some of the factories actually closed down and sent their girls to work at the Town Hall, and paid them as well. When we consider the political colour of this Council and the wonderful way the business houses helped us, I for one, strong politician as I am, thank them from the bottom of my heart for the way they came to our assistance. . . . During that week politics were unknown in Shoreditch, and here I want to commend the minority party for the help they gave us and for taking their orders from me, as though they were members of the Labour Party.[16]

By the end of September 1938 the *Gazette* reported that air raid wardens at Hackney had almost completed their house-to-house visits in order to fit all residents for gas masks. Across London there had been queues of people waiting to be fitted for gas masks as a consequence of the international crisis.

Hackney Council had employed men to dig trenches in the borough's open spaces such as Hackney Downs and Hackney Marshes, despite a national shortage of tools. The Deputy Town Clerk, Mr Dudley Sorrell, put out a special appeal for local people who had picks, spades and other useful tools to bring them to the council depot in Graham Road. Some 2,535 yards of trenches were dug; kerb stones were painted

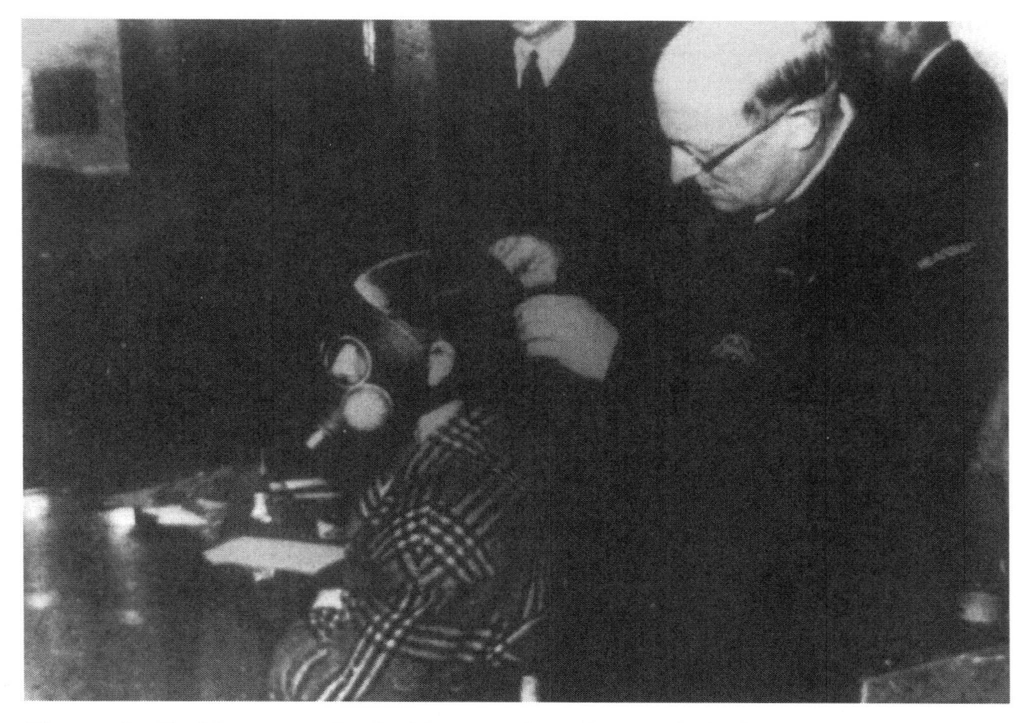

Thousands of residents were fitted with gas masks in the months leading up to the outbreak of war.

white; glass on all roof lights in libraries were blacked out; tens of thousands of sandbags were distributed. The owners of private cars and motor cycles were asked to register at the ARP Headquarters in Mare Street to act as dispatch carriers.

The Home Office had instructed the excavation of trenches but was apparently not explicit about their intended use. It was thought that trenches were to be used by people out on the street at the time of air raids, but the press pointed out that the number of trenches dug would have accommodated more than half the population of Hackney! Night watchmen were placed on guard to stop people falling in and were ordered to stay on guard until the Home Office told Hackney Council what was to be done with the trenches. By the beginning of October, *The Recorder* announced:[17] 'Trenches for 100,000 people finished . . . and no one knows what they are for.' The uncertainty over the value of trenches was part of a wider reassessment of the direction of ARP planning, focusing on two issues: the concentration of protection against gas attack and the cost.

The cost of ARP work was a constant bone of contention between the local authority, who were anxious to have in place a comprehensive service as soon as possible, and the Home Office, who would ultimately have to meet the cost of the work and were not anxious to invest in permanent and purpose-built structures, to meet an eventuality that might not occur. The question of cost crystallised in the debate over shelters. The Home Office had authorised a survey to be done of buildings that could be adapted

The Reading Lane side of the New Hackney Town Hall, heavily sandbagged.

as public shelters in 1938. However, in the opinion of R.H.R. Tee, Hackney's Town Clerk, 'the present position relating to the construction of shelters is too vague, and there is no precise instruction to the local authority as to the types of building that can be adapted . . . and how the cost is to be defrayed.'[18] More significantly, the underlying basis of ARP thinking was being questioned: 'the present scheme deals almost wholly with protection against gas, and there is, to date, no adequate provision made for protection of the population against the effects of incendiary and high explosive bombs.'[19]

The Town Clerk's views were echoed in the Left Book Publication *ARP*, by the eminent scientist J.B.S. Haldane, who had studied the methods of attack in the Spanish Civil War and concluded that the main danger came not from gas, but from high explosive bombs: 'The main killing weapon in Spain has been the high explosive bomb . . . Gas and incendiary bombs are subsidiary dangers. The same would be true if Britain were attacked. A considerable measure of protection had been given to civilians in Spain by digging underground shelters. The precautions so far suggested against high explosive bombs are useless . . . the policy of encouraging people to strengthen their own houses is impractical. Against air raids as against war, we need collective security.'[20] As a consequence of Haldane's observations and the growing view amongst people that undue emphasis had been placed on gas attack, the Communist Party and others actively campaigned for proper protection for the population in the form of deep bomb-proof shelters. It was argued that with no shortage of labour and resources, government policy should have veered in that direction. A deputation sought to have their arguments heard by Hackney Borough Council.

In September 1938 Hackney Council received a report from a member of ARP staff who had recently returned from a visit to Barcelona where he had inspected air raid defences. By the end of 1938 sections of the council were arguing for a change in the direction of ARP policy. In January 1939 the *Gazette* reported that Professor Haldane had led a bitter attack against the government at a public meeting on ARP organised by the Hackney Trades Council and Borough Labour Party at Hackney Town Hall.[21] A petition for deep bomb-proof shelters and other measures had been signed by many thousands of Hackney residents for presentation to the Home Office.

In April 1939 the Home Office rejected the mass construction of deep shelters, favouring instead the strengthening of basements.

However, Hackney Council pressed on with alternative proposals. By August 1939 plans had been drawn up for presentation to the Home Office for 168 concrete shelters at an estimated cost of £776,000, capable of offering protection for up to 92,000 people. Of reinforced concrete and brick built construction and based on the Barcelona model, these shelters were to be built 4 feet underground and were to be placed at strategic points around the borough. They were primarily for the use of people without back gardens who were expected to rely upon Anderson shelters. Authorisation to build was received from the Home Office in September 1939.

Preparation for war had continued in a planned and measured way in the months leading up to September 1939. Shoreditch staged a mock air raid in March in which

ARP personnel grouped at wardens' post number 3H.

hundreds of volunteers took part and pleas for further ARP volunteers and auxiliary firemen were made. Recruitment was slow as ARP work was not yet a reserved occupation. The natural target population was men of military service age who would face the likelihood of enlistment for the army as soon as war broke out. Nonetheless, the *Gazette*[22] was openly critical of the slow recruitment for ARP work in some streets in Hackney. ARP officers had complained:

> It is surprising to find that in the huge blocks of flats erected by the London County Council on the Pembury Road site only six persons have so far volunteered for ARP work. It is also beyond our comprehension why we have no volunteers from such thickly populated thoroughfares such as Wayland Avenue, Sigdon Road, Greenwood Road, Wilton Way, Dalston Lane (from Downs Court to Greenwood Road) and Graham Road (from the railway to Massie Road). Although as many as 22 gas masks have been delivered to residents at one house in Graham Road, not one volunteer has come from there yet.

But by the end of August the *Gazette* reported that there had been a surge of volunteers for ARP duty with all streets having a designated ARP warden. The German Hospital was set up as a casualty station after its patients had been discharged. The German staff were interned on the Isle of Man for the duration of the war. Trench

A warden emerges from the opening of the new underground wardens' post at the junction of Osbaldeston Road and Clapton Common, May 1939. Made of concrete, the internal dimensions measured a mere 16 feet by 16 feet.

digging took on a new lease of life under the direction of Herbert Morrison, MP for South Hackney, who was also chairman of the London County Council ARP Committee. He ordered that trenches be dug on all LCC estates in London. Women were among those who assisted in digging the trenches of the LCC flats at Lynmouth Road, Stamford Hill.[23]

The Recorder[24] reported that North London boys rushed to join the local territorials when they saw in the newspapers and heard on the wireless that boys who joined the Territorial Army that day would be exempt from Regular Army service. As a consequence there was a surge of recruits for the 5th (Hackney) Battalion Royal Berkshire Regiment. Eighty joined at the Hillman Street headquarters in Hackney and another twenty signed up at the Albion Road, Stoke Newington 'A' Company depot.

A mock aerial battle staged over Hackney Marshes attracted thousands of onlookers that summer with recruitment posts for the Women's Land Army, the Auxiliary Fire Service and ARP work.

On 9 August London staged a mock 'blackout'. These would become operational if war broke out. Crisis was looming again in Eastern Europe and the British government had been engaged in negotiation with the Soviet Union, but to no avail. The Soviet-Nazi pact was signed on 23 August. Britain reiterated that it would stand to defend Poland should that country be invaded and signed a treaty of alliance with Poland on 25 August. By 1 September Germany was bombing Warsaw.

By the end of August, the *Gazette*[25] reported that local ARP organisation was prepared for any emergency and that 'the workers in the various branches of National Service are ready to respond if the call comes'.

The call did come. Chamberlain's ultimatum to Hitler expired on the morning of 3 September. As soon as his announcement on the wireless had ended, the air raid sirens were sounding over London. They did not herald enemy aircraft but a single French plane, an indication of the 'phoney war' that was to follow in the months ahead.

The Schoolgirl's War – Judith Franks[26]

North Hackney, united in its desire for a new school could never, in its wildest dreams, have guessed how this new school was to be given.

On September 3rd, 1939, war broke out. But by this time most of North Hackney were already evacuated under the Government Scheme, and getting to know their billeters and the particular part of Hertfordshire in which they were billeted.

A few weeks later they were told that in future they would be going on alternate days to a 'new school' – just that. It was left to them to discover exactly how new it was.

They imagined every kind of school, but when the buses drew up before it on a fateful Monday morning, they saw what they are so used to seeing now – a beautifully modern building, one storey high, with an undeniable air of grace. Perhaps not quite the grace of the Georgian era, but definite grace in its low, symmetrical appearance and blending of straight lines and curves. Besides this, another important fact was noticed; it had an electric clock on the outside of the school. But, thought North Hackney, now that we are brought to school in buses, we cannot be blamed individually for being late. Why didn't we have it at the old school? Many an anxious latecomer would have been reassured if there had been a clock on the outside of North Hackney.

On entering the school, we found a large cloakroom with many improvements on the cramped ones at N.H.C.S. Then we were taken into the hall, huge and beautifully proportioned with French windows all down one side. And the people who lamented the lack of stage accommodation at North Hackney, perceived a fine platform with fixtures for curtains, footlights and wonder of wonders – a trap door (shades of Banquo's ghost.)

Our classrooms were apportioned to us and we proceeded to them through corridors of pale green and cream, very pleasing to the eye. The classrooms themselves were well equipped, light and airy, and some contained green roller boards, which had been seen at the Schools' Exhibition as the most modern of their kind. Chairs and tables instead of desks were the rule, and someone, mindful of a schoolgirl's disinclination to lift anything which can be 'shoved', had ordered little rubber discs to be put on the chair legs to subdue the noise.

Surrounding the school were beds of earth and a fairly big expanse of asphalt on which to run. But it will be noticed that no-one who is anyone in North Hackney runs after they have passed the first year; so decorous little groups could be observed discussing the merits and demerits of Buntingford School. The more adventurous ones went beyond the asphalt into the field which surrounds it and were delighted to find that they could not hear the whistle when it was blown. Tall, stately poplars mark the boundary of this field, and many of us when our minds should have been on our work, have tried to count them, or imagined them as graceful ladies dancing in the breeze.

But enough of meditation! North Hackney had more discoveries to make, more sights to see. At twelve it was time for dinner and we were once again marshalled into the hall. But what a different sight confronted our eyes! Three long tables laid with 'eating implements'. We filed down to our seats and after saying Grace, sat down. We received our dinners in strict rotation, each table taking its turn, and having its own direction. No collisions occurred, and after dinner, one hundred and eighty well-fed schoolgirls could be observed laughing and talking in the grounds.

There is still one thing which has not been mentioned; one might almost say the most desired and the most appreciated. Have you guessed it, gentle reader? Of course it is the gymnasium, a wondrous place with a well-sprung floor which makes the lightest tap sound like the rolling of thunder. But this was not its sole possession – there is also a wealth of gymnastic apparatus never dreamed of – wall bars, window ladders, ropes, booms, all designed to ensure that North Hackney grows up tall, straight-backed with the agility of monkeys. This thrilled North Hackney from the veriest babe to the most hardened Fifth Year.

In all, Buntingford School seems without peer or blemish, but many are the times when one thinks, 'I wish I were back at North Hackney'.

CHAPTER 4

The Calm before the Storm

The period from September 1939 to April 1940 was an anti-climax compared with the fervent activity of the months leading up to the declaration of war. Although the merchant navy came under attack from Germany's U-boats and there had been skirmishes along the Maginot Line, the Home Front experienced no direct German activity. These months gave Britain the opportunity to consolidate the preparations for war. The Home Defence plans included 'blackouts', rationing, the evacuation from London, the extension of military conscription and the establishment of a Home Guard.

It is possible that up to one-third of the population was affected by population movement in September 1939 alone, as a result of either enforced evacuation of children and women, or the wealthier inhabitants of London moving mainly westwards to Wales or the West Country. Estimates indicate that London alone probably lost one quarter of its population during this period,[1] leaving behind those people such as the King and Queen, who made a conscious decision to stay in the capital, those whose only means of livelihood meant staying in London and the poor who did not have the means to go anywhere. The movement of people did not stop with British citizens. During 1940 more than 30,000 refugees were billeted with British families.[2]

Plans to evacuate children from London had been in hand since 1938 when an official committee had reported that official evacuation must be restricted to the 'priority classes' in order to prevent chaos. This would involve the billeting of millions of people from the towns to the homes of country people. Parents in inner London received the following instructions at the end of the summer term in July 1939 from the London County Council:

> If evacuation should prove necessary during the holidays, wireless announcements will be broadcast. Parents of children will wish to know at what time to send their children to school on the day announced for evacuation. Parents are asked to listen-in carefully for instructions. Children should be sent to school properly

Hackney evacuees, probably on March Station, Cambridgeshire.

equipped at 8.50am (ten minutes to nine in the morning) on the day that evacuation is to commence, whether this should be a week-day, a Saturday, or a Sunday.

GAS MASK CONTAINER Parents are strongly urged to buy containers for their children's gas masks. They can be obtained (price sixpence) at Woolworths and at other large stores. If they are not in stock, the manager of the store will procure them if parents ask for them. It should be clearly understood that the gas-mask will be damaged if it is carried in its cardboard box without any other protection. AND A DAMAGED GAS MASK IS OF AS MUCH USE AS NO GAS MASK.

CLOTHING The children who are going away with us should have the clothing stated below (in addition to that they are wearing, which should include an overcoat or mackintosh):

BOYS One vest, one shirt with collar, one pair of pants, one pull-over or jersey, one pair of knickers, handkerchiefs, two pairs of socks or stockings, night attire, comb, plimsolls, towel, soap, face cloth, tooth brush, and if possible additional boots or shoes and plimsolls. BLANKETS NEED NOT BE TAKEN.

GIRLS One vest or combinations, one pair of knickers, one bodice, one petticoat, two pairs of stockings, handkerchiefs, slip and blouse, cardigan, night attire, comb, plimsolls, towel, soap, face cloth, tooth brush and if possible additional boots or shoes and plimsolls. BLANKETS NEED NOT BE TAKEN.

Constance Charlton's home at 12 De Beauvoir Square following a direct hit on 14/15 October 1940.

> FOOD Enough food for the day of evacuation should be carried. The following is suggested: sandwiches (egg or cheese); barley sugar (not chocolate); apple; orange. NO BOTTLES ARE TO BE CARRIED. Children should avoid excessive drinking before they move off or during the day. REMEMBER: The best type of carrier for clothes and food is a rucksack or haversack.[3]

Evacuation from Shoreditch, Hackney and Stoke Newington commenced immediately. The Headmaster of Pitfield Street School, William Thoday, wrote to the *Hackney Gazette*[4] describing the successful evacuation to the country of some of his pupils.

The *Gazette* reported that the majority of the children and expectant mothers had left the borough. Shoreditch Council had decided to have only a limited clinic service at its model welfare centre on Kingsland Road.

A detailed account of the evacuation of the Stubbs family from 12 De Beauvoir Square on 1 September 1939, entitled 'Goodbye Home', is told by Constance Charlton (née Stubbs):

> London in the summer of 1939 seemed very quiet. Other people who were there at the time have the same recollection. There were disconcerting happenings.

Our Mother washed, scrubbed and cleaned everything in sight. We went on more visits than usual to see our grandparents and on three consecutive days our Mother took us to the children's zoo in Clissold Park. In the garden there was a concealed Anderson air-raid shelter which could be mistaken for a slightly raised flower bed. It was a great place in which to play. Indoors there were black out curtains and blinds and gas masks. And in the park outside the front door was the strangest thing of all, a huge barrage balloon. I had also discovered that the bed linen in the drawer at the foot of the wardrobe had been almost entirely replaced with sugar. I asked my Mother why and was told to keep it a secret. Only now have I broken my word.

On the morning of 1 September we rose early and got dressed in several layers of clothes including our winter coats, even though there was no sign that the good weather was about to break. We left the house laden with rucksacks and gas masks. There were three children, Con 7, Pam 5 and because the baby, Val, was only 10 months old we were to be accompanied by our Mother. As we walked down the steps of our house in De Beauvoir Square, my Mother said 'Goodbye home'. On 20 October 1940 the house was bombed.

Our Mother had never regarded punctuality as a virtue, and as on many previous occasions we arrived late at Tottenham Road School. A few officials in charge of the evacuation remained in the playground. They attached labels to us and said to my Mother, 'You're too late to travel with your own school, you will have to join a party from Caledonian Road.'

At Kings Cross Station we boarded the train with children from Copenhagen Street School. Most were very subdued. Few mothers were there. On the train Pam and I sat and did French knitting, then we left that to stand at the window of the carriage and watch the countryside speeding past.

. . . Mother said: 'Rugby, they've sent us to Rugby. The first place they'll bomb. We're going home tomorrow.' I knew that there was no point in asking her what she meant.

At Rugby we were gathered together and sat around waiting to be collected by our temporary hosts. Our Mother was sitting on a tea chest and we were by her side when a lady came along handing out food. We were very hungry and cream crackers sounded like a real treat. I had never had them before but I don't think I have ever been so disappointed as I was on discovering what they were. It was not an auspicious sign.

Eventually a young woman arrived, smartly dressed, wearing lipstick and high-heeled shoes. She seemed impatient. 'Mrs Pollard is your host for the next few days, Mrs Stubbs' said the official. 'She'll look after you.'

We followed Mrs Pollard hurriedly past red brick houses until we came to a long wall. At the end of the wall was a door through which we passed, then we made our way across two or three back gardens and entered Mrs Pollard's house via the kitchen. This seemed very odd. Whilst we could come in by the back door of our house in London we never did.

In the living room a young man was combing his hair in the mirror over the fireplace. He turned round as we arrived. 'This is Mrs Stubbs from London' said Mrs Pollard, then, looking at my Mother, 'you can call him Shirley, Shirley Temple, we all do. It's the curls.' Mr Pollard was quite the most handsome man I had ever seen, tall, sun-tanned, blue-eyed, even white teeth, and beautiful golden curly hair. Mrs Pollard said, 'Bring your things through here' and directed us to the front room which, although it was still quite light outside was in almost total darkness. I imagine it was permanently blacked out. The light bulb had either fused or was non-existent, perhaps as a safety precaution. 'There's cushions and blankets' said Mrs P.

We returned to the living room and Mrs Pollard said to our Mother 'I'm off out now. There's egg and bacon you can have, and you could do the same for Shirley.' Shirley looked up from the comic he was reading. 'Give these people something to eat. They've come a long way, and you're not going out without cooking my tea.' My Mother would go to any lengths to avoid rows and tried to say something like, 'Please don't worry about us . . .' but her words were lost in the exchange between husband and wife.

Grudgingly Mrs Pollard produced a meal, put it on the table and turning to my mother said, 'I'm going now. See that the washing up's done.' Minutes later, Shirley gave himself an approving look in the mirror and he, too, left. We didn't see him again.

My Mother never showed the least sign of how she must have felt. She set to washing and changing the baby. We washed up together and then all went in the front room for an early night. It was difficult trying to arrange cushions and blankets in complete darkness in strange surroundings, but somehow we managed. Next morning we were awake very early although there was no way of knowing the time. There were sounds from the living room and my Mother went to ask if it was convenient for us to get up, adding that she would like to wash the baby's napkins.

'Get up when you like' said Mrs Pollard, 'and while you're doing your washing you can do mine. You can tidy up as well.' Our Mother, a very mildmannered lady, managed to keep her temper and said, 'Mrs Pollard, I realise it is very inconvenient for you to have us, but we are not here from choice, and I have not come to be your housemaid.'

'Please yourself' replied our hostess, 'but you won't be going anywhere as I'm locking the back door,' whereupon she left the house, locking the door as she had promised. 'Don't worry' said our Mother, 'We'll go out the front door.'

Within a short time we were ready to leave this unfriendly house, taking with us all our possessions, including the washed but still wet napkins. How my Mother coped I do not know; there were no launderettes, no disposable napkins and no plastic bags. My Mother intended to send a telegram to my Father telling him to come and get us . . . but knew once we heard the news of the outbreak of war, that we would not be going back to London for some time. We spent one more night in Rugby and next day we were taken by coach to a more permanent address at Rothwell in Northamptonshire, where our reception could not have contrasted more with the one we had received in Rugby. We stayed there until November 1945.[5]

There were inevitably thousands of similar stories of evacuated children who suffered during their periods of evacuation. By contrast there were thousands of children who found themselves billeted on homes which were clean, sanitary and where there was enough food to eat. Social conflicts were built into the evacuation system. Evacuees often came from the poorer sections of society and from the most overcrowded priority areas. Both the social tensions and positive aspects of evacuation to Kings Lynn in Norfolk were identified by Mr Balk, Headmaster of Hackney Downs School:

> In a situation where masters and boys lived within a radius of about a mile from the centre of the town, the intangible but very real barriers between those who teach and those who are taught inevitably broke down, for the amount of informal contact was probably greater than the contact provided by formal meetings in teaching periods. Some members of staff took boys into their own homes.
>
> At the same time the evacuation period was one of obvious upheaval and confusion. Medical arrangements required careful organisation. Billeting difficulties were never completely solved. Most billets were satisfactory and many were very good. But social and class antagonisms inevitably arose between the country

Masters of Hackney Downs School in Civil Defence uniform. The school was evacuated to Norfolk from 1939 to 1942. This photograph was probably taken when the school was based at King Edward VII Grammar School, Kings Lynn, in 1942.

The front cover of the programme of a variety concert held by Stoke Newington Air Raid Precautions personnel, bearing the distinctive SNARP logo.

folk of the quiet Norfolk town and the boys from working class homes in north London.

In an interview with a *Lynn News* reporter, Mr Balk pointed out that the householders of Kings Lynn had not given the same degree of co-operation as those of Upwell, and stressed the 'unsettling effect' of this on the boys. He went on to say that it was pointless to apportion blame and yet many of the Hackney Downs boys had settled down well and thrived in their new surroundings. But others were bewildered and unhappy.[6]

SNARP, the Stoke Newington ARP magazine, sought to make light of some of the problems associated with evacuation with the following observations:

> A young evacuee boy was helping his hostess with her shopping by carrying the basket. When emptying this on her return home she remarked that there were a number of things in it that she did not remember buying.
>
> 'Oh' remarked the boy, 'don't worry about them, mum, I told you it wouldn't cost you much to keep me.'
>
> The younger children returning from evacuation are eyeing the Borough's sandbags hopefully. The Town Hall carriageway is expected to provide a splendid playground when they burst.[7]

But evacuation was largely a failure. By the beginning of 1940 half of those children evacuated and most of the mothers with children under five went back home, mainly because the anticipated bombing of the cities had not happened but also due to dissatisfaction with the foster home, homesickness and family solidarity.

Following the fall of France in 1940, the government sought to reintroduce the evacuation of children but there were neither sufficient parents prepared to register their children nor sufficient volunteers willing to offer a billet. Although over 100,000 schoolchildren left London in June 1940, there remained over half a million in London in September:

> I have stayed in the Blitz because I did not want to leave London without my parents, and – what are London's noises to me? I am a Londoner! I have stayed in the country several times and have found it quite pleasant in summer, but in winter it is cold, slushy and depressing. There is no gas, no water, no electricity – even less than in London after a bad night's bombing. It is altogether too quiet for me because I was born and brought up in the City of London.[8]

In some areas home education was used to fill the gap following the closure of the schools in the threatened areas but often older children were roaming the streets.

Pupils of the Emergency Elementary School using a temporary crossing on Downs Park Road on their way to Hackney Downs School. The school was requisitioned by the London County Council to provide a basic education for children who stayed in Hackney rather than participate in the evacuation programme.

As a consequence, the government had to face the decision to reopen the schools in the evacuation areas, an admission of the failure of the scheme.

The education of children suffered during the war years, many children falling through the net of a formal education. The difficulty in running a school in wartime conditions is described in the log book of Glyn Road Emergency School. Here is an extract from 1940–41:

30.12.40 School re-opened as emergency school having been in use as Rest and Feeding centre for homeless people, victims of air raids.

03.01.41 Number of children attending – am 62, pm 63. Roll at end of week only 70. Some of children attending on Monday last had returned to Daubeny Road.

10.01.41 By end of this week roll had risen to 265.

17.01.41 Fresh children arrived daily throughout week. Re-organised classes and applied for additional staff.

22.01.41 Mr Sewell and Miss Nicholls joined the staff. Re-organised classes 1 and 2. Boys into 3 classes and divided infants between Miss Cook and Miss Nicholls. Opened room B on top floor.

05.03.41 Mrs Camps joined staff. Roll now 483. Classes re-organised by forming class from more advanced infants and backward juniors.

10.03.41 Miss Dailey and Miss Catling absent. Office sent Miss Cleaver. Roll now 500.

17.03.41 Miss Catling, Miss Rogerson and Miss Cleaver absent. Mr Sedwell returned. Office sent Mr French as temporary addition. Roll now 520.

18.03.41 Miss Rogerson returned. Case of diphtheria in house. Swab of teacher's throat negative.

19.03.41 Talk to parents by Dr Sutherland on Diphtheria Prophylaxis. About 40 parents present.

20.03.41 Very bad air raid last night. Many children absent.

These early months of the war saw the introduction of rationing and the blackout. Angus Calder described typical domestic preparation:

> The good citizen, already preoccupied with gas-proofing one of his rooms with cellulose sheets and tape, or erecting an Anderson in his garden, had to rush to the shops to buy blinds, curtains, blackout paint, cardboard, drawing pins, brown paper or whatever could be used to seal his windows at night. (And if he was prudent, he had strips of sticky tape over the glass, to minimise the shattering effects of blast.) All these commodities rapidly became dear or unobtainable.[9]

The shop next to the bomb-damaged house at 292 Wick Road has a heavily taped window to prevent shattering. The damage occurred on the night of 16/17 September 1940.

Londoners were denied all street lighting and signs after dark, making life difficult for the pedestrian and the motorist. Car headlights were masked and trees and lamp posts along major routes were painted with bands of white paint, In September 1939 the number of people killed in road accidents dramatically increased. The numbers of casualties dropped only following the introduction of petrol rationing. If pedestrians took torches onto the street at night, the bulb had to be covered in a double thickness of tissue paper. Many pedestrians injured themselves at night by walking into objects or falling over dangerous paving stones. As a consequence many people chose not to go out at night preferring the relative safety of their homes where they could listen to the Home Service and the new Forces Programme. One programme which developed a cult following during the war was ITMA (*It's That Man Again*). For those Hackney people whose appetite for the cinema did not diminish in spite of the blackout, the *London Recorder* of 20 October 1939 reported the opening of the Clapton Ritz:

> The Ritz has taken a year to build. Its construction embodies all the latest building features. It will be absolutely safe during an air raid. Steel and concrete only have been used in making the building. All glass in the building has been sprayed with a special 'non break' solution which will not be affected by blast. It will neither blow into the cinema nor into the street. . . . Gas cannot enter the building. There are no sealed doors or traps to make the building air tight, but the Plenum air-conditioning plant does all the work.

During the war the Clapton Ritz suffered blast damage as a result of a direct bomb hit on an adjacent building but remained largely intact.

Policemen and ARP wardens would patrol the streets ensuring no light was visible from people's homes. Draconian fines were levied on people who disobeyed the blackout. A library porter was fined ten shillings for not closing the curtains of the public library at Brooksby's Walk.[10] Blackout rules were relaxed slightly by Christmas provided all lights were turned off when the sirens sounded. The cinemas, dance halls and sporting venues were reopened and were packed out. In February 1940 British summer time was brought in, to be replaced in the following year by double summer time which lasted for the duration of the war.

But despite these war-time measures on the home front, there was a short-lived belief that in the absence of any attack on Britain the war would soon be over. The population had been prepared for a war of gas attack and bombing but this had not materialised.

The 'calm before the storm' had given rise to growing discontent with the numbers of volunteer air raid wardens, rescue and demolition squad workers and the auxiliary firemen, who were being paid £3 a week in the case of a man and £2 for women to remain idle. It was argued that they should be replaced by the unemployed. The matter was taken up by South Hackney MP Herbert Morrison, who defended the volunteers' patriotism and citizenship.

Developments on mainland Europe were soon to alter people's perceptions with the first British overseas campaign. Following the Soviet invasion of Finland in the winter of 1940, the British and French governments decided to launch an expeditionary force to Finland via Narvik in Norway. On 15 April British forces had landed in Norway. By 11 June Allied troops were withdrawn from Norway after heavy casualties and without achieving their original objective.

In Parliamentary circles, the Allied offensive in Scandinavia was regarded as a shambles. Britain's poorly equipped troops were no match for the German army. Dissident Conservatives and the Labour Party viewed Chamberlain's resignation as inevitable. The question that then occupied everyone's attention was 'who would succeed Chamberlain?' It was increasingly recognised that the country needed a government of national unity. It was imperative therefore that Chamberlain's successor had to have the confidence of the Labour Party and the trade unions. The Labour Party refused to serve under Chamberlain. To the shock of Chamberlain's supporters, Winston Churchill was asked to form a new government and on 13 May 1940 Churchill, the great orator, delivered his first speech to the House of Commons as Prime Minister overseeing a national government with representation from the Labour and Liberal Parties, with a Cabinet that included the prominent trade unionists Ernest Bevin and Herbert Morrison, Member of Parliament for South Hackney.

By June 1940 the Low Countries and France had fallen to German occupation. The British Expeditionary Force had been cut off at Dunkirk and despite the great bravery of British troops and the hundreds of volunteers who took small boats over to France to rescue the stranded army, Churchill regarded Dunkirk as 'a colossal military disaster'.[11] Britain awaited the expected invasion 'Operation Sea Lion'. Britain was at its lowest ebb in the entire war.

Ten months after the declaration of war, Britain and the Empire stood alone against Germany ready to face the attack that would surely come. Churchill and his military advisors calculated that the key to repelling a German invasion would be air superiority of the Channel.[12] The long awaited air war commenced in July 1940.

In attempting to knock out the British war machine Hitler was hopeful of a British surrender without the need of invasion. On 19 July in an address to the Reichstag Hitler announced:

> A great Empire will be destroyed, an Empire which it was never my intention to destroy or even to harm. I consider myself in a position to make this appeal since I am not the vanquished begging favours, but the victor speaking in the name of reason.[13]

Hitler's appeal was rejected within the hour. On the night of 1 August the Luftwaffe dropped the text of Hitler's speech across southern England. On 2 August Goering ordered the destruction of the RAF.

During this period no enemy action had occurred over the three boroughs although there were nightly reconnaissance flights by the Luftwaffe. However, the emergency services were put to the test on the night of 11 August 1940 when a Spitfire crashed at the rear of a baker's shop at the corner of Chatterton and Blackstock Roads. The pilot had successfully baled out and Stoke Newington went to the assistance of their Islington ARP and fire fighting colleagues.[14]

In the period from late August to early September, British defence systems came under sustained attack from the Luftwaffe. The loss of British fighters in the air and on the ground outstripped production from the factories. By 6 September the RAF had suffered a heavy loss of pilots and the first civilian bombing on the city and the eastern suburbs of London had occurred on 24 August.[15] The RAF retaliated and bombed civilian areas of Berlin, confounding the promises of Hitler to his people that they would be free of such attacks.

Goering was growing impatient. An invasion of Britain should occur before winter. He estimated that British fighter loss was so great that there was little air defence left to repel an invasion. By 7 September 1940 a mass of shipping was waiting on the other side of the Channel for the delayed invasion of Britain to commence.

In those hot summer weeks of August and September one of the greatest air battles of the Second World War was staged over the skies of southern England. Although the pilots of the RAF sustained great loss of life and aircraft, the German loss was greater. There is no doubt that despite the months of sustained bombing that followed those weeks of the Battle of Britain, it was the fighter pilots of the RAF, ground defence troops and the war production workers that prevented the invasion of Britain by Germany in 1940. Hitler was not given another opportunity to invade Britain for the rest of the war.[16]

One of the first war-time incidents. Mr Roberts and his family from Shoreditch were all in their Anderson shelter when their home was destroyed on 31 August 1940.

CHAPTER 5

The Blitz

On 7 September 1940 German strategy changed from one of invasion to an attempted knock out blow of London.

It was a fine, sunny afternoon. At about five o'clock vast numbers of hostile planes made their way up the River Thames from the east. There were some 375 bombers whose intended target was the dock area. They made their way westwards as far as Kensington. The Thames corridor was ablaze from the dock areas to the City.

Daytime bombing allowed the Luftwaffe a clear view of the target. It also allowed British defences an uninterrupted view of the aggressor. As a consequence, this was the only daytime attack upon London throughout the period that came to be known as the Blitz.

Ted Harrison describes his memories of that day:

> I remember looking out from my verandah and seeing the German planes flying over in formation, about twenty of them and there were a couple of our fighters after them. I thought, Good God, it's 1916 all over again! I'd seen these planes the Gothas coming over after the Zeppelin raids in the First World War. And when I saw these Junkers, I thought, blimey, we've lost the war. I wondered how they could have flown over in broad daylight. When they came back at night you could see the glow from the docks.[1]

The Luftwaffe returned by nightfall and inflicted sustained bombing on London until 4.30 a.m. the following morning. By the time they withdrew, the scale of fire was apparent. There were nine conflagrations which appeared unstoppable, nineteen fires that demanded more than thirty pumps, forty ten-pump fires and nearly a thousand lesser fires. It was the dockside boroughs that suffered the greatest number of deaths and destruction of factories and homes. Three of the London railway termini were put out of action. That night 430 men, women and children lost their lives, deaths mainly caused by the impact of collapsing buildings and flying glass.[2]

Inspired by curiosity, crowds gather around a small crater on the edge of Victoria Park on the morning of 8 September 1940.

By contrast, the scene on the same morning at Cressett Road was one of devastation.

The Luftwaffe returned the next night, extending their operations to the City proper and by Monday morning all the main line railway stations to the south were out of action. On that night 412 civilians were killed and 747 severely injured.

The majority of bombs that fell on the three boroughs during the Blitz were either high explosive ranging from 100 pound to 4,000 pound, incendiary bombs or oil bombs. The first oil bomb recorded in Hackney fell on the night of 8 September 1940 on the Middleton Road railway bridge. Many bombs did not detonate on impact but nonetheless caused considerable damage through the momentum they acquired, fracturing gas and water supplies and shattering windows. Considerable destruction was also caused by anti-aircraft shells from our own defences. One previously unknown weapon which fell upon Hackney was the parachute mine. This was a bomb with a parachute attached, which in the early days of the Blitz was mistaken for a German parachutist.

On Monday 9 September the raids were extended beyond the Thames corridor and the City with all inner London Boroughs under attack. On this night 370 people were killed.

By the end of the week Londoners knew they were under siege. By the end of September the capital had been bombed every night and 5,730 people had died. By the beginning of October Germany declared the bombing campaign as a war of attrition. London endured fifty-seven nights of continuous bombing through to 2 November 1940.

Crowds wait to gain access to Liverpool Street underground shelter: During the height of the Blitz, the tunnels from the station could accommodate up to 10,000 people in very unsanitary conditions. Later in the war; a new shelter was built which could accommodate 1,000, with water-borne sanitation, bunks, a medical post and sick bay. (Imperial War Museum, HU 49507)

Pressure upon the authorities forced the opening of the tube stations as places of night shelter and these became the refuges of many Londoners that autumn.

People from Shoreditch used Liverpool Street and Old Street underground stations. The tube stations were regarded as safe and secure despite an incident at Bank Station in January 1941 when a bomb tore into the road above the station causing water and masonry to fall onto the shelterers below. One hundred and eleven people died. An uncompleted railway extension from Liverpool Street ran underground eastwards and could accommodate 10,000 people. Fierce competition for underground places grew and petty criminals would extort money from people for reserving pitches. Besides sleeping on the platforms people resorted to sleeping on the escalators once the power supply had been turned off. Hammocks would be slung over the rails. Some homeless people in the Liverpool Street shelter stayed underground for weeks. If homeless and jobless they had no need to ascend to the surface and there was no compulsion for them to do so. Needless to say, parts of this shelter became unsanitary and harboured germs and disease. Mosquitoes and lice spread unchallenged. A week into the Blitz, the government set up a committee to examine public health in the shelters. It had reported by the end of September 1940, but its recommendations for proper supervision and medical facilities were not put into practice until the end of the Blitz.[3]

The Reverend H.A. Wilson of St Augustine's in Haggerston, describes in *Death over Haggerston* a night spent in the Liverpool Street Tube deep shelter by one of his parishioners:

> It is 5.30 on an evening in October. Thanks to the time-bomb in Yorkton Street I can't go into the Priory tonight, so I must start getting ready to go down to the tube. I collect a cushion and a blanket, to make myself as comfortable as possible; cut myself a few sandwiches; fill a bottle of water; walk down the street; board a number six bus; take a three-halfpenny ticket to Liverpool Street Station a mile away.
>
> I get there about 6.0 to find that what appears to be the whole population of East London has arrived before me. However, I manage to reach the stairs that go down to the platform, and get down them fairly easily; as a matter of fact, I couldn't have fallen if I had tried – too many people were wedged round me, and they carried too many soft parcels and bundles of bedding.
>
> On the platform are police and porters in plenty, to tell us that we must not stand beyond the white line, so that passengers may be able to get in and out of trains. I look around. The Hebrew race is well represented, and each descendant of the twelve tribes is determined to make himself or herself as much at home as possible. Mattresses, blankets, pillows, alarm clocks: they have brought everything except bedsteads (and hot water bottles aren't needed in the tube). If you get into conversation with them, they will tell you that they have been waiting outside in the street for most of the day, and have been down there since 2.30 in the afternoon; so you can guess what sort of a chance a late-comer stands of getting a resting place.

> I stand for hour after hour: as do many others. The heat is terrific. I am glad of my bottle of water, and wish there was a little something in the water.
>
> I find myself looking forward to the arrival of a train, as it brings with it a current of air that is perhaps fresher, and anyhow is of a different sort. Time passes. A porter shouts that we can now get to our places. The next moment I am swept from the platform to the escalator. Someone tells me to push and shove and run like everybody else. I manage to sit down on my bundle. It is two o'clock; I have been on my feet there for eight hours, and I am a woman who has done a day's work.
>
> I sit there and watch others in some marvellous way find a place to stretch themselves out in, and so settle down for a few hours' sleep. Time creeps along, somehow. I hear no sound of bombs or gunfire, which is some consolation. But I find myself thinking rather longingly of St Saviours Priory, of the nice hot cups of tea and cocoa handed round, of the space and airiness, of the Sisters untiring in their efforts to make us as comfortable as possible.
>
> The night slips on; I must have dozed, five o'clock is getting near. Then a policeman wakes sleepers, tells us all that trains will soon be running, and that spaces on the platforms must be cleared again for the passengers. I am grateful for a quiet night; but it is good to be out in the fresh air even of Bishopsgate. I walk home to Haggerston for a little sleep before another day's work begins; and hope, as I see a rope across the entrance to Yorkton Street and the notice DANGER UNEXPLODED BOMB, that the Royal Engineers working in the garden of number forty five will be kept safe from danger and will get the horrible thing up before another night comes.[4]

Damage by bombing was exacerbated by gas and flooding and Councillor Alman, the chairman of Hackney's Civil Defence Committee was forced to appeal to all householders, factory and business premises owners to turn off water, gas and electricity supplies when air raids were in progress. Failure to do this had caused extensive damage to property and extra work for the hard pressed civil defence and fire fighting services.[5]

The Duke of Kent visited Hackney in September 1940 and toured the areas destroyed by enemy action. The *Gazette* reported that he talked with many people made homeless by the air attacks. The borough's billeting officer, Mr C. Webb, was reported as having had to deal with over 14,000 enquiries for accommodation.[6]

The most terrible loss of life in the three boroughs in a single incident occurred on the night of 13/14 October 1940. People were sheltering in the basement of a building which belonged to the Four Per Cent Industrial Dwellings Society known as Coronation Avenue, situated at 157–61 Stoke Newington Road. A heavy bomb fell upon the building destroying all five floors and blocking all the exits from the shelter below. A water main burst flooding the shelter and fire broke out in the debris, One hundred and seventy-three people lost their lives. The memorial to the incident in Abney Park Cemetery lists the names of those killed, many of whom were of Jewish origin. The *Hackney Gazette*, for reasons of national security, understates the incident in its report and seeks to play up the morale of the onlookers:

West Hackney Church was destroyed by enemy action on the night on 18/19 September 1940.

> On Friday the King and Queen, with whom was Admiral Sir Edward Evans, paid an informal visit to an area where there had been casualties owing to a bomb demolishing a block of tenements underneath which was a shelter.
>
> Accompanied by the Mayor, their Majesties quietly toured the neighbourhood to inspect war damage.
>
> Arriving at the damaged flats, they watched the rescue and demolition workers and men of the Pioneer Corps at work, and chatted with relatives of raid victims and several of the flat dwellers. The crowd sang 'God Save the King'. Both King and Queen expressed their heartfelt sympathy for those who had become casualties and their thanks to all who had helped in rescue work.
>
> Several men and women who recognised their Majesties called out 'God Bless You!' and as they were leaving the crowd sang the National Anthem. The King was in uniform, and Her Majesty wore a costume of dove grey.[7]

At the end of the working day, shelter life took over:

> The time is six o'clock in the morning. I have just woken up and wondering where I am, I find myself in the shelter. The two people who live upstairs have

> become tired of waiting for the 'All Clear' and have gone into the house. My father has just got up and is emerging from the shelter door. Having shut the door, we are now on our own, my mother, brother, and myself. Soon father comes down with an inviting jug of tea. Having drunk the tea, my brother and I decide to get up and stretch our cramped legs. We leave mother alone in the shelter, and go into the living room where a warm fire is blazing.
>
> It is almost seven o'clock and the 'All Clear' has gone. We switch on the wireless and are just in time for the news. By the time the news is nearly over, mother walks in. I start washing myself and then have my breakfast and prepare for school and go out. At first sight everything seems to be all right, but on turning the corner I find the remains of three houses. The HE bomb which destroyed these houses had fallen when we were in the shelter, too near to be comfortable. I went further up the street where about a score of buildings were rendered useless. A bomb had fallen in the middle of the street here and blown the inside out of all these houses, and so I continued to school.
>
> During school hours three or four warnings went. Three o'clock came and four hours later the all-night warning. It all depends what sort of night it is. If it is clear and light we go into the shelter. If it is a bad night with pouring rain we take our chance.[8]

Sybil Palenbaum, a second-year pupil of Laura Place School, recalled a near miss on her house:

> The sirens had gone and all the household was in the shelter. Bombs were falling, guns were firing, but all the same we were snatching a little sleep, when all at once, we were awakened by a terrific rumble and a whistle. We clenched our teeth and waited, thinking a bomb was coming for the house. Suddenly, there was a terrific medley of loud crashing, glass breaking and screaming. We all thought our house was gone, but on looking out, after a horrified pause, we found not a grass garden, but a glass garden. Wardens rushed in and told us to go to the church hall as they thought an incendiary bomb was on our roof. So we collected a few things and made for the hall. There we had tea and tried to sleep until morning. Next day, we returned home to find our house was still there, but a mine had demolished three shops.[9]

The night raids continued throughout November, but on the 14th the enemy turned their attention to the city of Coventry. Although there was a heavy attack on London the following night, thereafter the raids on London became relatively lighter, the Luftwaffe turning their attention to the bombing of other British cities and ports. There were however some exceptional nights. At the end of December the City of London suffered incendiary bombing for over three hours. The result was mass destruction by fire with St Paul's Cathedral surrounded by flame but emerging virtually unscathed. Hackney and Shoreditch suffered badly on the nights of 27 and 28 December. Cecil Sindell, manufacturer of lanyards whose factory was in Middleton Road, Dalston, recalled:

Residents and Civil Defence workers pick over the ruins of flats in Downs Park Road, 1940.

A Royal Air Force crew arrive by lorry to assist the rescue parties at Downs Park Road.

A pavement enquiry point and food office set up following the Downs Park Road incident

A Salvation Army canteen provides refreshment for the rescue workers at Downs Park Road. The lorry on the left contains tarpaulins for temporary housing repairs.

Mangled Anderson shelters following an incident in Chelmer Road on the night of 24/25 September 1940.

> We had a lot of air raids round here; yes we had a mine linked . . . a bomb linked to a mine which dropped at the top of Middleton Road; and quite a lot of people were killed. Fortunately at the factory I had iron framed windows and they were very small and the factory really took the blast away from the houses in Malvern Road, but windows in every house pretty well were smashed in because it was a 500 pound bomb and there were two big explosions in quick succession. And we had one a few doors away from here dropped on an air raid shelter and 4 people were killed, and all their belongings were hanging on the wet trees, looked like a Christmas tree in the morning with their belongings there, very sad. And Middleton Road all the way through caught it very badly. The factory had an air raid shelter, we had two shelters, that could take 50 people in each and both of them were used to keep the staff in two separate areas and everybody did their fire guard duty at night time. I slept more at the factory than I did at home: everyone had tin hats and gas masks . . . the only time we stopped was for a fortnight when the gas mains were blown up, and we were forced to put motors in temporarily 'cos our gas engine was stopped.[10]

It was not until the nights of 8 and 9 March 1941 that the Luftwaffe reconcentrated their efforts on the siege of London. On each of these nights over 150 bombers

The scene of destruction in Middleton Road following the bombing of 27/28 December 1940 described by Mr Sinden.

The aftermath of a second bombing of St Matthews Hospital, Sheperdess Walk, on the night of 20 February 1941. The hospital had already been attacked on 8 October 1940 when many invalid, elderly residents and staff were killed.

attacked, killing over 200 people. This was doubled ten nights later when 300 planes attacked, causing 751 deaths and over 1,000 injured. These two nights saw the heart ripped out of Hackney. The *Gazette* describes the 'Nazi's orgy of destruction' but again deliberately understates the destruction and deaths involved to comply with Ministry of Information orders:

> ... Only a matter of yards prevented the Narrow Way in Mare Street, Hackney being included in the wreckage of a recent raid. As it was, it was the wider part of the thoroughfare adjoining Hackney Railway Station that sustained the greatest damage. The Railway Tavern was so badly shattered that it is now undergoing total demolition. On the opposite side of the way, between the Old Tower and the railway bridge, the site of what was a small row of shops and other buildings – including Broadribb's, the chemists and the coal office of C. Miller, two of the oldest in the borough – is today completely vacant. The Tower itself is minus its clock, though the stone masonry seems to have stood up well to the blasting it received; but the Midland Bank in front was practically gutted and the cottages in Bohemia Place nearby were damaged beyond repair. Shops adjacent to the Railway Tavern suffered varying degrees of damage, and I understand that among the fatal casualties were Mr Day, manager of Sanders the Jewellery firm, who was roof fire 'spotting' and Mr Griffiths, manager of the billiards hall above the railway station entrance. St John at Hackney Rectory was damaged by blast. Incidentally, the Rector, the Rev. N.A. Robathan, is still on active service – he was among those evacuated from Dunkirk – and his brother who is carrying on in his absence, was fortunately not spending the night at the Rectory when the bombs fell. [11]

Across London, the nights of 16 and 19 April witnessed an appalling loss of life. Over 1,000 deaths occurred on Wednesday 16th and as many on the 19th. It is probable that the severity of these air raids was in direct retaliation for the renewed bombing of Berlin by the RAF.

The last and worst of the great bombings of the Blitz occurred on the night of 10 May. On a clear night over 300 bombers dropped their loads over a five-hour period. This night saw the greatest number of recorded casualties, 1,436 dead and 1,792 injured. The scale of destruction was terrible. Famous public buildings were hit as well as the cheaply built and easily destroyed homes of the dock areas. But on that night the RAF with the help of ground defence gunners was able to destroy thirty-three enemy bombers, which probably accounted for at least one-tenth of the enemy capability as it was known that the Luftwaffe bombers would each make more than one excursion each night over London.[12] After this the scale of the bombing raids diminished, with the last raid of the Blitz occurring on 27 July 1941.

The main concentration of bombing fell upon the dock areas, Stepney, Poplar, Bermondsey, Southwark, Deptford and Bethnal Green and the City. The areas of Shoreditch and Hackney and to a lesser extent Stoke Newington, were badly affected because of their close proximity to these areas. The Metropolitan Borough of Hackney

The destruction of central Hackney between the Old Church Tower and the railway bridge following the bombing on 19/20 March 1941.

recorded in photographs the extensive bomb damage that affected the borough throughout the war and probably produced a record of every incident. Shoreditch sustained greater damage to homes, businesses and civic buildings such as St Leonard's Church, but many of the Shoreditch war-time records have not survived.

It would appear that initially the Germans sought to strike at the heart of Britain's commercial, industrial and political base, but as the Blitz continued, the bombings became the gratuitous slaughter of the civilian population in an effort to break the morale and will of the British people. The loss would have been significantly greater had it not been for the exacting work of the emergency services, the volunteers and individual acts of heroism that abounded.

The ARP Man's War[13]

One of Hackney's ARP wardens was Mr T.E. Browne whose private diary provided a background to the work he and his colleagues undertook. Here is his entry for 17 October 1940:

Warning in morning at 8.20 which delayed me getting to work slightly. The evening raid started at about 7pm. Mum and Doris were in [trenches?]. Dad, Elsie and I in Anderson shelter. Planes coming in from the north caught the barrage and we heard two bombs whistling down, but not the long whine, from the moment it left the plane, just a short 'e e e bang' in each case. The shelter shook and debris could be heard falling for a few seconds. Obviously near, so I jumped out of the Anderson and saw smoke and dust across the gardens. Quickly I unbolted the brick gate, ran along to Cleveleys Road (the next turning) and as the dust was so thick it was almost impossible to breathe. I turned and ran for the Post to report. Met Mr Friswell outside my own house as he was running up, asked him to send in an Express Casualty for this end of Cleveleys Road (there being no fire) and ran back again. The air had slightly cleared, but I could not see one side of the road from the other. A young man in front of me said, 'I think it's over there' – pointed to the opposite side of the road. Over we went and saw a pile of debris. I lost him, but clambered over what I found out afterwards were the roof rafters laying across the crater, and yelled out 'Is anybody there?' – a voice answered 'here warden'. I went over the ruins into the back gardens and helped out some people who were in the Andersons, quite unhurt but shaken. Could not see anybody, as dust was still thick. I went round the gardens enquiring and found a young Jewish girl rather hysterical half out of her shelter. She said her mother was trapped in her house. I went in and found Mrs Neale of Post 11 (next door neighbour) in what was left of the room in which was a bed containing an invalid woman. She was not at all frightened and did not want to be taken to hospital as she said she was only laying there wanting to die. But as the house was wrecked I told her we should have to take her to safety. Just then the S.P. arrived and we all got her out. I then saw Mr Pinter and he wrote to the M.I. and ran away with it (he had seen a soldier on the way to the Post and ran back with him). The ambulance was ready and just as the invalid was going to be loaded into it, Mr Rigby of Post 11 came round and

The incident in Cleveleys Road, described in Mr Browne's diary on 17 October 1940.

asked for it as he said he had casualties in Gunton Road. This was the first I knew of the other part of the incident. Of course I said I wanted the ambulance and got rather excited so I asked the advice of the S.P. leader who said the other casualties were more urgent, so I sent in a report for another ambulance.

While I was dodging about I heard Sherman's voice yelling out 'Browne' but I had to ignore him for a time. I sent for the incident lamps and flags. The other ambulance arrived and when I looked round for the invalid she had gone but nobody knew where and as the ambulance then arrived I sent it round to Gunton Road as I knew they needed it. Then Danny Cohen said he had seen some people taking her to Beaumont Court. I went off the deep end and enquired why the f—— he let her go without telling me and what was the Incident Officer for etc and blamed his lack of training. I heard a long time after from a man in the [trenches] that the soldiers took her away, so Cohen was not altogether in the wrong.

I was about to send in a supply report for another ambulance to take the woman away from Beaumont Court when the S/C car driver said he would take his car back as it was not needed, get an ambulance and take the woman away. I said it was not according to regulations but we both agreed that regs were made to be broken.

Mr Ayers? was on the scene for a short time but a locally resident police officer (afterwards we heard he was some big noise – Inspector Sorrell from J Division) sent him away as he said he was drunk and smoking. This scandal is being hushed up.

Mr Browne and ARP colleagues.

I got the rescue people to have a look around the adjoining houses, and when they and the S.P. said they had no other work to do, I dismissed them. They were all pleased with the speed of operations which took only 1 hour 20 minutes from start to finish.

I then went round the houses enquiring as to where the occupants of the shelters had gone, as I had to make provision for their being homeless. I could get no information so went to the trenches. Here I found three homeless (one was the husband of the invalid) but they were quite comfortable for the night and I told them to enquire at the Post for the address of the Rest Centre in the morning. I also heard that the homeless had been sent away from Gunton Road in an ambulance as Ridley must have done this without telling me.

That finished my work so I returned to the Anderson to sleep. In the morning I passed the incident on the way to work and marvelled at how I had been clambering back and forth over that lot. Luckily it had been dark and I couldn't see for dust. Tried to phone Post from office during morning. . . .'

CHAPTER 6

Heroes

When the heavy bombing of the Blitz started most of the volunteers for the Auxiliary Fire Service (AFS) had never experienced fire fighting. Their first experience came on the night of 24 August 1940 when nine major fires were started around London including a one hundred pump fire at the Bishopsgate Goods Yard. These fires were declared uncontrollable and spreading and the novice fire crews had to continue exhausted until the fires were under control or they could be relieved by the next shift the following morning.

When the first major attack occurred on 7 September the dock areas of Stepney and Poplar were prime targets. Fire fighters were confronted with not only the difficulty of overcoming the fire, but also the chemical reaction of the items stored within the warehouses. The Ministry of Information pamphlet *Front Line 1940–41* describes some of the effects:

> In the docks strange things were going on, as they did on many nights thereafter. There were pepper fires, loading the surrounding air heavily with stinging particles so that when the firemen took a deep breath it felt like breathing fire itself. There were rum fires, with torrents of blazing liquid pouring from the warehouse doors/and barrels exploding like bombs themselves. There was a paint fire, another cascade of white-hot flame, coating the pumps with varnish that could not be cleaned for weeks. A rubber fire gave forth black clouds of smoke so asphyxiating that it could only be fought from a distance, and was always threatening to choke the attackers. Sugar, it seems, burns well in liquid form as it floats on the water in dockland basins. Tea makes a blaze that is 'sweet, sickly and very intense'. It struck one man as a quaint reversal of the fixed order of things to be pouring cold water on to hot tea leaves; . . . a grain warehouse on fire brings forth unexpected offspring – banks of black flies that the firemen's jets wash off the walls, rats in hundreds and as for the residue of burnt wheat, 'a sticky mess that pulls your boots off'.

A scene from the London Fire Regional Control Room on 14 December 1939. As appliances moved from one district to another; so these women from the Auxiliary Fire Service moved the pegs on the mall map. (Imperial War Museum, HU 36128)

During the first twenty-two days and nights of the London Blitz, the regulars of the fire service, the auxiliaries and men and women brought in from the regions had attended nearly 10,000 fires. Fighting fire on this scale required considerable organisational skill; the allocation of fire-fighters, the route to each fire, made difficult by impassable streets that contained bomb craters and rubble, allocating the correct number of pumps to deal with the size of the fire, and ensuring that there was a supply of water as the mains water piping was frequently damaged. Often the women in the control rooms had to judge which fires should be given priority over others. By August 1941 the government came to recognise that it was impossible to organise fire fighting across separate locally controlled brigades and formed the National Fire Service.

Alongside the fire services were to be found the ARP services (the term Air Raid Precautions was changed to Civil Defence in September 1941) who acted as the eyes and organisational brain of the rescue services. It was the ARP patrols who recorded the 'incident' to the control centre and if fire had broken out, to the fire control. The controls then ordered out ambulance, fire crews and rescue crews to remove the dead and to rescue those people who were buried in collapsed buildings. The warden then returned to the incident to account for the inhabitants of a house or the population of a street and to direct the medical services to help the shocked and injured. ARP personnel were all drawn from volunteers and most were employed in regular jobs. All had undergone extensive training under the direction of the local authority and were known and usually trusted in their neighbourhoods, although some were said to have attracted resentment through their own self-importance. ARP wardens were officially employed for a maximum of seventy-two hours a week but this was usually exceeded at the height of the Blitz. There was twelve days annual leave. The men were paid £3 5*s* a week and the women £2 3*s* 6*d* a week. One in six of all wardens were women. Most wardens had paid employment elsewhere and would arrive on duty after a day shift or after the housework or child rearing. They were usually middle aged or even elderly. The official role of a warden was described by government as follows:

> Street wardens will be required to act as guide and helper to the general public in the area to which they are allotted. It is particularly important that they should help to allay panic and give assistance to any families and persons in their districts e.g. those who may have been driven out of the houses etc. They should help to direct people in the streets to the nearest shelter. They should report to the Police or the local intelligence centre the fall of bombs, dangerous fires, presence of gas, blocking of roads, damaged mains, and any other information that may be required to enable a particular situation to be dealt with. They must be trained to give accurate reports and to assess the situation.[1]

But the life of a Civil Defence worker was not always as straightforward as official parlance directed:

> Tracing the casualties was a never-ending anxiety. How many were there, and where had they been? The householders were supposed to let the warden know where they would spend the night. But they forgot, or they changed their habits. If the bomb fell during the evening, there might or might not be friends with them. Under that formidable heap of brick and timber there lay how many human beings unconscious and in pain? Perhaps fire was creeping forward and minutes were precious; had they been sitting in the kitchen, at this end of the house, or in the parlour, at the other? Where should work begin on the debris of the great block of flats. That injured little boy mustn't be taken away before he tells where his granny and sister were sitting when it happened. Did anybody see the caretaker? Is it true the old couple have been going to shelter lately and weren't here at all?[2]

The Shoreditch ARP control message documents for much of the Blitz have survived and reproduced here is one official report of a bombing incident at Chatham Avenue on 8/9 September 1940:

02.24	Report of H.E. bomb, Chatham Avenue between Nile Street and Murray Grove.
02.28	Report of casualties.
02.37	Report of casualties trapped under wreckage.

02.45	Ambulance sent.
02.51	1 stretcher bearer to St Leonards 1 ambulance to Chatham Avenue.
03.00	Civilians from bombed houses brought into City Road Police Station; also one expectant mother.
03.31	1 party returned from Chatham Avenue. 3 cases to hospital, 1 sitting case to no. 2 F.A.P. Reported impossible to continue work on account of fire.
03.35	1 ambulance, 1 car returned from Chatham Avenue. Present strength 4 ambulances, 3 cars.
03.35	1 party back from Chatham Avenue. All suspected casualties out. Scrutton Street rescue party arrived. Fire raging on site. AFS attending.
03.38	One ambulance returned from Chatham Avenue.
03.42	4 parties returned from Chatham Avenue. Total casualties 1 dead, 4 to hospital, 1 walking case, 8 sitting cases to no 2 F.A.P.
04.00	Reporting party 2 back from Chatham Avenue. Job completed.
04.03	5 persons under debris. Rescue and demolition party required.
04.14	1 ambulance returned from Chatham Avenue.
04.25	1 party returned from Chatham Avenue. Not allowed to approach incident owing to fire.
04.32	Rescue party has arrived at Chatham Avenue but there are no trapped casualties.
04.36	Gas pipe fractured. Gas escaping.
04.46	RSD have gone – informed by Fire Officer that at present nothing can be done. Fire too furious.
04.50	2nd party returned from Chatham Avenue. Warden says no casualties trapped here but he had asked for 5 motor pumps.
11.10	Coping very dangerous. Require R.S. EMERGENCY.
12.15	Mr Clayton of St C warden's service is at Chatham Avenue and suggests that Borough Surveyor should survey damage, give permission for tenants of 7 blocks to return to their homes.
16.50	Send 1 party to Chatham Avenue. Mr Hayward visited incident and required urgent attention.
16.55	Two ambulances to be sent to Chatham Avenue, scene of last nights incident.[3]

Perhaps the work of the ARP warden is appropriately summed up in an anonymous poem entitled 'W' which appeared in SNARP:[4]

Who is it who for long months past
Has to his many tasks held fast,
And helped along the great solution
Of the Gas Mask Carton Distribution?

He upon whom the public pelter
Questions regarding their Anderson shelter,
Who has often turned out at the end of the day
To collect up the forms and file them away.

At all monthly meetings his presence would show
To fire up his questions right from the word go,
And although the Major would set a fast pace
He would never be found the last one in the race.

He who at present is on the alert
The guard of the public – to keep them from hurt,
And now who to sport his effort has striven
Lest to great physical strain he is driven.

Who is this man who never does shirk
The irksomest duties – oft tiresome work,
His name I won't mention, you surely have guessed
For work and for service, he's one of the best.

London could not have survived without the other regular and volunteer forces comprising rescue and first-aid personnel, ambulance drivers, control staffs, telephone operators, the police, the Home Guard, messengers and those men who worked around the clock to repair gas and water mains, telephone cables and the electricity supply.

At its first meeting following the commencement of the Blitz, Hackney's Civil Defence Committee reported that the borough had suffered severely from enemy air attack but were able to report that all civil defence personnel had carried out their duties magnificently. The committee praised the arrangements made for billeting the homeless. Several hundred people were helped by the organisation set up at Central Hall and staffed by council and voluntary workers. The London County Council set up a communal meals service staffed by volunteers for those people who could no longer cook at home because of disruption to gas or electricity supplies. Seven such kitchens were set up in the three boroughs at Millfields School, 96 Upper Clapton Road, Homerton Row School and Lady Holies' School, Scawfell Street, Laburnum Street and Stamford House in Stoke Newington High Street. Meat and two vegetables cost 6*d* and a pudding 2*d*.

Where children were attending school, the authorities sought to provide them with school dinner:

A Hackney ARP social event, 1939. This was one of many such events held during the war and would have been attended by all Hackney organisations involved in Civil Defence.

Civil Defence workers with colleagues from the Home Guard.

> Homerton Road Centre (a rest centre for 'bombed-out' people) caters for the mid-day dinners of four schools in Hackney, and we are fortunate to be one of these. The dinners started in January 1942, with a steady average attendance from Laura Place of fifty children. By the kindness of Mr Connolly, the supervisor, we were allowed to have a room to ourselves, thus enabling us to organise our own Dinner Scheme. There are nine tables and a serving table. These are covered with pretty American cloth but Miss Hole wished it to be as home-like as possible, so table-cloths were obtained and are washed at the school every week. On Mondays, therefore, the tables look most attractive covered with their clean linen. This was especially the case during the spring days when each table had on it a pot of flowering daffodils. This earned us the name of the 'Ritz' from the Rest Centre staff.[5]

In the British Restaurants, run by the LCC, people could dine cheaply without the use of ration coupons. Two eighteenth-century rooms in houses in the grounds of the bombed Brooke House were converted into a British Restaurant during the war and meals continued to be served there until 1946.[6]

Mobile food canteens were also provided. The trustees of the Eton Manor Charitable Trust at Hackney Wick provided £300 to provide a mobile canteen for the use of civil defence workers, bomb disposal units, fire-fighters and others.

The scale of possible homelessness had been underestimated by the authorities.

Rescue workers enjoy a tea break at a mobile canteen in Wick Road provided by the Eton Manor Cadets.

A canteen serving rescue workers, first-aid parties and members of the public at the Eton Mission, Hackney Wick.

In the nine months of the London Blitz over one million houses in London had been damaged. If houses had been rendered uninhabitable, people would stay with family and friends wherever possible. Billeting schemes existed but the numbers of homeless far exceeded supply. The homeless poured into rest centres, mainly empty schools and other public buildings. On 28 September 1940 a special Regional Commissioner for the homeless was appointed to oversee the organisation of the rest centres. Staff with social work training were appointed and better equipment provided to cope with the need for sanitary arrangements, mass feeding and clean and secure sleeping accommodation. In the meantime, billets were sought and lightly damaged houses were made good to enable the former occupants to return. For the rest of the Blitz, the numbers resident in the rest centres fluctuated in proportion to the bombing raids.[7]

Hackney was at the forefront of dealing with the aftermath of bombing attack. The *Evening Standard* of 26 October 1940 was full of praise for local organisation but recognised that the council was unable to do all that it wished to:

> Hackney was the first borough to centralise all the various applications arising from raid damage. To-day I saw the system in action. In a large hall previously

used by the Salvation Army a hundred people were filing through. They were drawing new identity cards, new ration cards, receiving immediate cash to compensate for goods destroyed, arranging for the council to move furniture from their wrecked homes.

The billeting officer, Mr Charles Webb, said that during the first week of the raids people, often only half clad, had to trek from one part of the borough to the other – here claiming cash to carry on, there a new identity card and somewhere else filling in a form assessing the damage done by bombs.

It was at his suggestion that all these claims were dealt with centrally.

The Council now have another problem to solve; the storing of salvaged furniture. Every available building in the district is filled. Nothing remains but church halls and although these are empty the council have no power to requisition them. So somebody's furniture must remain on a pavement or in a half wrecked house until somewhere has been found to put it. Both Mr Webb and the Borough Engineer Mr Cyril Helsby, feel that much might be saved that is being lost at the moment. Mr Helsby thinks that all clothes and bedding should be recovered as soon as it is safe to approach the bombed houses. They should then be laundered and kept until claimed.

We walked up a street of damaged houses. In one an old man was coming down a rickety staircase, dragging a carpet after him. There were already several

A Womens'Voluntary Service enquiry post at Daintry Street, Hackney Wick. The WVS personnel refused to be photographed saying it was against rules. They hid in the doorway on the right while the photograph was being taken.

chairs on the pavement. 'When I get this lot out, and the geyser, on which I have only two more payments to make,' said the old man, 'I'll be satisfied.'

In another, a soldier was searching among the ruins of his home. In the ruins of a grocer's shop the proprietor was digging for his bank book and insurance policies.

In the roadway there were mattresses and bedding, sodden with rain, but otherwise undamaged.

Helping the homeless, the bereaved, the shocked and the destitute became the domain of the Women's Voluntary Services (WVS), who often staffed the rest centres, mobile tea and food canteens and offered their services to anyone in need. Drawn mainly from solid middle class stock they assumed a prominent position in the volunteer movement on the home front. The work of the Stoke Newington WVS was praised in the 7 November 1941 edition of the *Hackney Gazette*:

> The Stoke Newington WVS which had been carrying on its manifold war activities at Stoke Newington Library has this week moved to more commodious quarters at Stamford House, Stoke Newington High Street. The branch has played a prominent part in tending to the requirements of those whose

The Millfields Light Rescue 'A' shift making toys for the Hackney Day Nurseries in 1942.

> homes have been destroyed or damaged as a result of enemy action; the caring for and teaching refugees staying temporarily in the borough; tackling the problem of evacuating the under 5's; giving out clothing, collecting coupons, doing knitting, sewing, ironing and mending and performing other useful services. . . . His Worship, the Mayor acknowledged with gratitude the services rendered by the WVS in the troubled days following the 'blitz' and the splendid work they had done and were still doing for the war refugees from abroad, who in Stoke Newington had found a home from home. . . . The WVS had also done much for the people who had been bombed out in the borough. On every occasion when their services were required they had come to the rescue. Not only had they clothed these people, but they had shown them human sympathy, making the way more pleasant for people who had been in dire trouble.

The WVS had a major role in clothing distribution and it organised a 'Housewives Service' for women, who worked alongside the local ARP workers by checking lists of names, making tea for casualties of air attack and providing general help and

Queen Elizabeth inspects Stoke Newington's Civil Defence capability on 23 May 1940.

comfort. In the latter part of the war, the WVS was instrumental in setting up a distribution exchange of goods provided by the people of Shropshire to the people of Hackney.[8]

Public support was given freely to the volunteers who courted danger to help the population. The *North London Observer* recorded that over 5,000 people attended a Home Guard demonstration in Clissold Park in the summer of 1943.[9]

In September 1940 the King introduced the George Cross to mark acts of heroism for which purely military honours were not appropriate. There was no shortage of local recipients. 'Stoke Newington proud of its heroes' was a headline in the *Gazette* on 26 February 1941. The story read:

> Two men who performed acts of heroism, recognised by the award of the George Medal, were introduced to the members of the Stoke Newington Council on Saturday. They were Mr John Cochrane Easthope, chief assistant in the Council's Engineer's department and Leading Aircraftsman R.S. Prior of 33 Kersley Road.
>
> The Mayor said that when a large number of people were trapped in a public shelter Mr Easthope entered the middle compartment through a window, in spite of the danger of the total collapse of debris and the fact that water was then about four feet deep, and worked his way over and under the debris in an endeavour to rescue anybody who might be there, but primarily to carry out a reconnaissance on the spot. He found debris blocking the centre compartment up to a distance of 15 feet from the point of entry. Several persons were pinned under the wreckage, but Mr Easthope entered again through the emergency exit into the north compartment, where water was several feet high and appeared to be rising. Regardless of the danger of being crushed or of being trapped and drowned he made four separate visits while searching for trapped people.
>
> The Mayor then presented Mr Prior, who he said, was the son of a servant of the Council. While on leave Leading Aircraftsman Prior showed conspicuous bravery by entering an aircraft which had crashed and caught fire in the street where houses were immediately adjoining, the pilot having descended by parachute. A gun in the aircraft was firing to the danger of people in the vicinity and ammunition was exploding.
>
> In spite of the danger of the petrol tank exploding, he removed the back plate of the gun and stopped it firing. His hands were considerably injured. He attended the First Aid Post where his mother was engaged and there his wounds were dressed.

Similar stories of gallantry followed in the press in the following weeks. The *Hackney Gazette* of 24 March carried the story 'George Medal for Boy Costermonger':

> Four Dalston police constables and a Dalston costermonger – 16 years old John Cain have been awarded the George Medal for the part they played in a 'blitz' incident a few months ago. Cain, who was only 15 at the time, is the youngest of a family of 13. His home is at 172 Hindle House, Arcola Street. The police

The burnt out premises of Reeves and Sons, artists' colour manufacturers of Ashwin Street, Dalston. Four police officers and fifteen-year-old Sohn Cain received the George Medal for rescuing men trapped in the basement of the bombed factory.

officers are: George Hubert Dean, John William Turner Mead, Roy Victory Edward Slowley and Ernest John Tricker.

The awards are in respect of the bombing on November 1st last of the premises of Reeves and Sons, Ltd. artists' colour manufacturers in Ashwin Street, Dalston. The official record of the incident is as follows:

A paint manufacturers' premises received a direct hit and soon the whole building was ablaze. The police constables arrived and were joined by Cain. He knew that several people were trapped in the private basement shelter directly underneath the fire. The party separated to find an entrance. After being repelled several times by smoke and heat, they all eventually found their way into the basement, having to pass through burning wreckage, paint, water and live electric wires. Part of the basement had collapsed and several men were trapped. The debris and everything around was running with oil paint. . . . The officers and the boy Cain speedily freed six men from the wreckage, and carried them on doors and planks to ambulances. A few minutes after the last of the six victims had been removed from the basement, the whole interior of the building collapsed.

> A *Gazette* representative who on Saturday visited Ridley Road Market, where Cain's mother has a vegetable stall, found that he had been called away to Hackney Hospital where his father was reported to he seriously ill. He is believed to be the youngest holder of the George Medal. At birth he is said to have weighed only two and a half pounds and his mother put him in cotton wool. He was then fed with a fountain pen filler.

Other acts of courage resulting in commendations were reported in May 1941 in the *Gazette*:

> Two Hackney and two Stoke Newington ARP workers are to receive the George Medal for gallantry in air raids. They are JOHN FOSTER, lorry driver, attached to the ARP rescue service, Hackney.
>
> When bombs demolished houses many people were trapped. Foster immediately joined in the rescue work and crawled into a small cavity in the wreckage, where after breaking through a door, he reached five victims. He was giving aid to these when the debris collapsed and he also was trapped. When the other members of the squad reached them they found Foster protecting a woman from the falling rubble by holding his steel helmet over her face. Although dazed and bruised, he extricated three women who but for his untiring efforts, would undoubtedly have been suffocated. By his efforts seven persons were rescued.
>
> EDWIN VANDERLEIT, plumber of the ARP rescue service, Hackney
>
> When people were trapped under wreckage of houses, Vanderleit was lowered into a small hold where he found a woman and supporting her with one arm, gave her refreshment which was passed down through a tube by a doctor. Other members of the squad then worked to reach Vanderleit and the trapped woman. This took four hours owing to the loose and dangerous state of the wreckage. During this time Vanderleit continued to support the casualty and protect her from the slipping debris. He displayed outstanding courage and devotion to duty and through his efforts the woman was extricated alive.
>
> FRANCIS HARLOW TRITT, leader, and JAMES WOOD, member of the ARP rescue party, Stoke Newington.
>
> A high explosive bomb wrecked a house and a family was buried. The mother was pinned from the waist downwards by a collapsed floor only a few inches above her head. Tritt, assisted by Wood, cut a way down to her. The two men started digging with small shovels and uncovered the heads of a son and a daughter. Another member of the family was pinned down by the leg of a bed on one shoulder and a fireplace on the other. The leg of the bed was sawn away and the weight of the fireplace taken off his shoulder. In order to release the mother and

> son much of the debris had to be scooped into buckets by hand. Several times further falls reburied the casualties, but eventually they were extricated. After further digging in steadily worsening conditions the daughter was also released. Tritt and Wood next began to get the remaining victim out but constantly falling debris made this extremely difficult and dangerous. Tritt used his own body to shield the injured boy and after 11 hours work the rescue was complete. Tritt and Wood by their gallantry and devotion to duty saved the whole family.

No doubt there were countless other examples of bravery and self-sacrifice which went unrecorded and unrewarded. People did what they had to do to save themselves, their families and friends, their neighbours and total strangers. They did so without considering the cost to themselves. People volunteered to place themselves in these often highly dangerous situations. It has to be said that they were all heroes.

The Councillor's War – Florence Davy (Née Sills)[10]

When war was declared it was decided to have an emergency arrangement whereby four members of the council would run the affairs of the borough. This consisted of Councillor Loweth, a Tory, and three leading Labour members, although it was a completely Labour area. Alderman Goodrich presented this idea to the rest of us but I was against it. I was the only one. As I was a lone voice it was agreed, but it didn't last. When councillors realised they were members in name only, they also realised they knew nothing and were not consulted, so it came to an end. I became a member of the Civil Defence and Finance Committee and campaigned for deep bomb-proof shelters. My husband was an architect and the architects and surveyors were doing their best to promote deep bomb-proof shelters. At that time we were providing surface shelters and strutted basements apart from the Andersons in people's back gardens. Mine was again a lone voice but as the intensity of the air raids on Hackney grew greater a change took place. I was in the Town Hall on a night a land mine was dropped behind it. When we had meetings we had to stay. It was impossible to get home. On this particular night we had to keep the iron door open to avoid being entombed if the Town Hall came down. The blast came right down one side of the building. All the windows were shattered but fortunately the building stood.

People were trapped in strutted basements. If the building above was wrecked burst water pipes drowned them, fractured gas pipes suffocated them and if the people died from shock they remained standing or sitting or whatever until they were touched and then they would fall down. On the night the bank at the corner of Coronation Avenue, Stoke Newington was bombed, we lost four hundred people in strutted basements. By March 1942 I was sent out of London by my doctor. I was exhausted and had been too closely involved in too many bombs. I had been going all over the place. I went to Harrogate to my relatives and almost immediately started to work for the Ministry of Aircraft Production. I continued to visit London when I had my breaks.

The deep bomb-proof shelters were eventually built. They were built on all open spaces and they were safe. We had them on Millfields and all open spaces of that kind. And we had wardens who patrolled them. The behaviour was good and it was a safe place where

A deep bomb-proof shelter under construction in 1944 on the site of the Hackney Baptist Chapel.

people went every night. About six o'clock at night you would go there. As soon as you got the first warning you went to the shelter. We didn't really come out until after six in the morning and then we would resume the day. We lost all our windows, we mostly had our roofs stripped off by blast if the house remained standing. But once the windows were gone, they were just boarded up. We didn't have windows any more so when you were indoors you had the light on. But most of the day really, you were trying to get your shopping because you had to queue up for everything, you see. If you saw a queue you stuck yourself on the end of it and then you asked what the queue was for. If it was something you wanted you stayed and if you didn't want it you went away. But of course in addition to that you kept yourself scrupulously clean, especially your feet because if you were picked up in the street, it would be a terrible disgrace if you had dirty feet.

I remember one particular instance in the early part of the war when of course the planes just circled overhead all night and then just dropped their bombs before they left to intimidate us and they only dropped about 50 pounders. But once they had taken Dunkirk they loaded themselves up on bigger planes with their land mines. Now there was one that dropped on Gunton Road. Now the strange thing about land mines was that somehow or other the effect of the blast would kind of skip and then attack something a little way away, not immediately near it. And there were two young couples in Beecholme Road and they decided they were fed up going to shelters. They were not going to do it. So this particular evening they were in an upstairs room and they were playing cards, because boredom did get you and sometimes you did stay in your bed. Anyway they were there when this land mine went off. The whole of the back of the house fell out and the wardens who were running to the scene heard these cries.

One of the shelters constructed by Hackney Council. Situated in Bayford Street, the shelter withstood the impact of air attack on the night of 22/23 September 1940, whereas the adjacent houses at numbers 3 to 9 did not.

These people had been blown up onto the roof of the house next door and they hadn't got a stitch of clothing on. They were clinging to the roof calling out for help. There were instances like this that were really rather funny. Also as a result of that, someone a little further along the same road, opened the door and found they had got a complete wardrobe in their garden. It was undamaged and it was full of clothes and later on in the morning a man came round and said 'I understand that you have got a wardrobe in your back garden' and they said, 'yes'. He said 'I think it's ours.' And he had a look at it. And it was his and it was the only thing that he had got left. The whole of the house and everything had been completely destroyed and they had lost everything but the wardrobe had sailed over two rows of houses and landed safely in the garden.

Shelters were dug in all open spaces, especially Millfields and residents took nightly refuge there. These proved to be adequate and apart from a touch of scabies now and again, I wouldn't criticise them.

In 1937 I became a candidate for councillor in a bye-election. You were selected by the local party as a candidate on a ward by ward basis. Although I lived in Upper Clapton, I stood in Clapton Park because there was a bye-election and the Labour Party agreed that I would be the candidate. There was a change then from a Conservative Council to a Labour Council. It was predominantly Labour and it has been ever since.

I was often a lone voice and I could often be a thorn in the side of a chairman of a committee and the leader of the Council who I didn't particularly like. Anyway, I stood for what I stood for and I was proved right. I had to stand very often on my own in the Council Chamber and I was very young and inexperienced but I did it. When we had local people coming forward to petition for deep bomb-proof shelters and because they were led by the Communists – now this didn't make any difference to me because there were all kinds of organisations involved there, but it was the principle of it. And it was a principle that I was fighting for. But I was the only one on the Council and I had to try to introduce them. It was the night of the inauguration of the new mayor, Tommy Gooch, and he didn't thank me for keep getting up. But I got up altogether five times to try to get this deputation to be heard and the fifth time he bought the hammer down and said I would be escorted from the chamber if I got on my feet once more. Locally, I had tremendous support. In the Labour Party I had tremendous support, but eventually my health broke. We didn't go to bed at night and sometimes when you went into a shelter you could only sit on a seat and you sat there all night, and you had to go on the next day and the next day and it just went on and on.

When the first phase of the bombing was over, we had of course, the flying bombs. So long as you could hear it, you used to listen, you were safe. The moment it cut out, you had to dive, and if you had nowhere else, you then laid in the gutter against the granite kerb as protection. After the flying bombs, we had the rockets. If you heard a rocket then you were safe. They would carve down into a building and the people who were left stranded up on the floors for some unknown reason would throw themselves down. It was a shock reaction. It was very dreadful. I remember at that time that we had been on public libraries. We had the libraries repainted. It was 1944. We tried to smarten them up. I don't know if you ever knew the library we had at Dalston. It was a lovely library, a centrepiece. On this Saturday morning, we went round and saw and inspected the libraries. We went in there, we spoke to the staff. Staff who we had a long time in that library and we spoke to them all and had a pleasant time with them. On the Monday, it was all wiped off the face of the earth because the rocket fell on it and we lost the staff, we lost the building, and the Vicar's wife from St. Philip's Church was there and one or two other people. Apart from that it was just the general raids. When you came out from a council meeting the next morning there was no transport because the roads were strewn with broken glass and rubble. You would just walk over it, climb over it. But during the course of the day it would all get cleared up. The first thing, before you came out of the shelters, the air raid wardens would go round the sites. Where people had been blown to pieces they would pick up the pieces and they would put them in a sack. So you never saw anything like that. The public morale was so important that every care was taken to keep it high although there were certain instances where a number of people died and they had to bring them out and lay them on the pavement until they were taken away. But generally speaking you didn't see dead bodies or parts of bodies. That was all taken care of before you came out of the shelters. The fire service did a magnificent job. They were terrible times.

CHAPTER 7

Business and Industry in the War

British rearmament had commenced in 1935 with a programme which in theory was to produce an air force on a par with the Luftwaffe. The British Navy also underwent an overhaul. It was the army that was in a state of parlous neglect, having been geared primarily for home defence. Germany spent £1,710 million, equivalent to 25% of her gross national product, on armaments in 1938. By contrast Britain spent £358 million or 7% of gross national product.[1] Until Munich, Britain's expenditure on an effective war machine had been strictly limited by the Treasury and, to some extent, by pacifist public opinion. After Munich, rearmament spending escalated, with the economy being geared to war production.

In recognition that Britain had no further military allies in Europe who were free of German domination, the new National Government under Churchill conducted a fundamental policy shift. Economic prudence it was felt could not win a war. As a consequence spending on the war soared to a weekly average of £55 million. The economy totally embraced war production. Engineering factories commenced around the clock production. Normal working hours were abandoned. Ten- to twelve-hour shifts became the norm. Production rose by one quarter in the period which followed Dunkirk. However, by 1941 it was recognised that long working hours were causing exhaustion and ill health. As a consequence a limit of a sixty-hour working week was placed on women and Ernest Bevin, the new Minister of Labour, advised that the same weekly ceiling be placed on male workers.[2]

The unemployment of the 1930s had turned to full employment by 1943. Conscription into the armed forces and into essential areas of war work meant a national shortage of labour. Many people had two jobs. Women swelled the numbers of the employed by undertaking full- and part-time work according to individual circumstance. As the war machine grew it became quickly apparent that there were insufficient men of working age to expand both the armed forces and factory production. The competition for and the rising price of labour brought about the entry of women into the labour force in bigger numbers than had ever been the case in the past. Hackney's first day nursery at the French Hospital in Victoria Park Road opened its doors to 50 children in April 1942.[3] Conscription of unmarried women aged between twenty and thirty into the armed forces had been introduced in December 1941. Thousands of people volunteered for work in the munitions factories in their spare time. Full employment led to a corresponding increase in wages. Those employed in the engineering industry saw skilled rates of pay extended to the semi-skilled who had undergone training.[4]

The government had to recruit labour from overseas. Forty thousand Irish people were recruited to the munitions factories and by the end of the war one hundred and thirty thousand Italian and ninety thousand German prisoners of war were working for the British war effort.[5]

The government took an incremental approach in introducing controls over raw materials, prices, labour and retail outlets, but eventually was able to regulate production to prevent 'unessential' goods being produced.

Despite the bombing and conscription into the armed forces and the movement of personnel away from 'non-essential' into 'essential' war work, local business and industry sought to continue to operate against all the odds. Many of the larger local companies suffered severe bomb damage. Some were able to ride out the storm due to the dedication of employees and the remarkable co-operation of companies who came to the rescue of their competitors in times of difficulty. Others suffered severe disruptions and looked for new premises in safer parts of the country away from the heaviest bombing.

Shoreditch, a major centre of the furniture industry, played a significant role in the production of austerity furniture and in essential war work:

> Many furniture makers fought in World War II. Those who did not were either allocated to war work (mainly done by the larger firms), the production of Utility furniture (mainly done by 'middling' sized firms) or reconstruction work (done by the very smallest firms). Stocks of timber were so great when war broke out in 1939 that there was no apparent shortage of furniture for some time. Two days after the declaration of war, the Ministry of Supply imposed timber control regulations under the Defence of the Realm Acts. By July 1940 all timber supplies to the furniture industry ceased. Production continued to some extent from stocks of timber already held by manufacturers. As shortages increased, so did profiteering. Price controls were brought in by the Government in an attempt to regularise matters. Purchase taxes of a sixth to a third were introduced on many goods, including furniture, to reduce demand as well as raise revenue. Demand however rose as half a million or so marriages continued to take place each year. The price of second hand furniture went through the roof.
>
> In 1941 the Utility Furniture Scheme was introduced which emphasised good design and the economical use of timber. Utility furniture was only available to newly-weds or people who had been bombed out of their houses and lost all their belongings. Prospective buyers had to get an application form from their local fuel office for a permit. Each permit carried 60 units and was valid

for three months . . . public meetings were held at which designers of Utility furniture made serious attempts to find out what people needed and how furniture was used.

For the small family firm making furniture, the war brought hardship for those who were judged unsuitable by the Government for war production or the making of Utility goods. Some were lucky to be appointed as repairers, undertaking what was called reconstruction work which involved using old furniture and wood to make 'new' pieces. Ray Hille, who by this date had taken over from her father, Salaman, found work assessing bomb-damaged furniture after the firm's Old Street premises were completely destroyed in December 1940. New workshops were obtained in nearby Rivington Street where several of the older employees rejoined her as the firm began the repair of bomb damaged furniture bought at auction. Other firms simply closed as family members joined the forces or else they went into necessary war work. . . . All the wartime production in East London was carried out in circumstances which were, to say the least, far from favourable. Many furniture makers were bombed out of their homes as well as their workshops yet, somehow, they managed to obtain makeshift premises, to beg or borrow tools and materials and carry on despite the odds.[6]

One Shoreditch firm, R & J Hill, purveyors of tobacco, was completely destroyed by enemy action in May 1941. After 150 years of manufacture in Shoreditch, the company was determined not to give up. The site on Shoreditch High Street was cleared and a ceremony took place a year later attended by the Mayor of Shoreditch to mark the intended building of new premises. John Davenport's history of the company describes the scene:

And now you are to picture, please – a fine day in Shoreditch. No longer a distinguished borough in the social sense (84,000 people live in its one square mile) but industrially one of the most important boroughs in all London.

We are in the High Street. On both sides are symptoms of Hitlerism, here and there: boarded windows in many hues of old cardboard, blank red-rimmed gaps where offices have been burnt right out . . . on a great open site some acres in total extent, paved neatly enough with broken bricks, a lawn has been made: new turf; a little sand and gravel pathway, and everything, just between what is still Shoreditch High Street and what used to be (it runs along the middle of the cleared space) Spencer Street, now Anning Street.

On a corner of the new laid lawn, which is itself a tiny corner of the stretching site, is a green kiosk. It looks lost enough in that vast expanse, but there it stands, for all Shoreditch to see as it passes by: the beginning of fresh things, a brave continuance of the old. It will rebuild itself – is doing so already . . . the land is bought and the plans are being drawn. Here after many vicissitudes this very considerable tobacco undertaking will still be administered, will go on making its two mixtures for the King's ships, its cigars for the House of Peers, as it has done for many a year now, and its cigarettes for the likes of us that are neither Kings, Peers nor sailor boys.[7]

As manufacture geared itself to the war economy, firms were instructed by government for war production. Nalder Brothers and Thompson, manufacturers of measuring instruments based in Dalston Lane carried out work to government specification.[8] The paint manufacturers, Berger, turned over part of their production lines to the manufacture of anti-gas paints in 1939. The company suffered the bombing of the varnish and other departments on the night of 8 September 1940, but production recommenced a few days later with the assistance of a competitor company, Indestructible Paint and Varnish of Park Royal. Help was also on hand from Messrs Mander Brothers who provided Berger with vital supplies of varnish and dry colour paint.[9]

The bombing of Bergers on that night is described in the company's official wartime record:

> The warning went at 4.57 pm and we then witnessed for the first time a large formation raid over the Docks. It was from this experience that Mr King decided together with Mr Heighington that different arrangements would have to be made with regard to the question of Spotting, as it was felt that our Spotting Posts were in such a vulnerable position that had such a raid taken place over Hackney, our fire watchers would not have stood any earthly chance. It was indeed fortunate that this change was carried out. The same evening the factory had an extremely narrow escape when an HE (high explosive) skimmed the main gates and fell into the open ground opposite where the NFS water tanks are now situated. This was considered to be serious enough, but within 24 hours we were to have a bomb all to ourselves. This fell at 11.10 pm on Sunday night, September 8th, 1940. It has never really been determined whether it was an HE or an oil bomb – it was felt that the latter was the more probable. It can be said that it was a perfect hit for Jerry as it fell right in the centre of our varnish storage tank rooms containing over 100,000 gallons of varnish, together with a few thousand gallons of other inflammable materials. . . . Our own fire brigade had two branches operating within two minutes of the missile falling. This obviously needed outside help, and the AFS were summoned – over 100 pumps were used, and the fire took eight hours to extinguish. It must be recorded here that whilst the AFS had been criticised and had their legs pulled during the preceding year for their comparative inactivity, they really did do a marvellous job of work. This fire endangered the whole of the works, and all Berger voluntary personnel were in action at different parts of the works extinguishing hot embers, cooling down the roofs etc., thus avoiding the total loss of the factory. One serious result, other than the fire was the severe flooding of the basement of location 100 including the control room, but despite everything Miss Ward, our ARP telephonist, stuck to her chair with her feet up in the air, with tar and water flowing around her, and the place completely in darkness except for emergency lighting.[10]

J.G. Ingram and Son, the London India Rubber Works, of Hackney Wick was also turned over to war production:

> During World War II, Ingrams were able to give all their skill and experience to the production of goods and materials for the alleviation of suffering and the saving of life. Field dressing stations and hospitals from Normandy to Stalingrad, from Norway to El Alamein, all received from Ingrams a continuous flow of the finest quality surgical rubber appliances. Enormous quantities were sent, through the Ministry of Supply, to all our Allies. Ice caps, air cushions, water beds, hot water bottles, field dressings, syringes of all kinds, serum caps and vaccine caps for all the thousands of war time inoculations – these are only some of the essential supplies turned out by Ingrams during the war.
>
> In most of the factory departments, peace time work on articles such as sports equipment and other non-essential goods ceased altogether, while production of feeding bottle teats and other domestic lines were greatly reduced, and later, when rubber was in short supply, came almost to a standstill. However, this did not mean any slackening of the pace of production. There were many new and urgent requirements for the Services, the Ministry of Supply and the Ministry of Aircraft Production. In the sports goods department, in the hot water bottle and general mechanical goods shops, the management changed over to production of a new and vital material – the self sealing rubber covering for the fuel tanks of bomber and fighter aircraft. The greater part of the teat shops was turned over to covering bomber tanks. In the 'spreading shop' one section was soon working at top pressure on materials for aircraft fittings such as fuel hose or sealing strip for emergency doors and gun turrets. Other shops produced goggles for the RAF, the Royal Navy and Service Transport; gloves for the protection of workers on chemicals, and explosives and miscellaneous mechanicals for a hundred and one purposes. When Malaya was lost to the Allies, Ingrams performed a special service for their own and many other factories, in washing to a high standard of cleanliness the African wild rubber that, in its crude and dirty state, proved such a problem to all manufacturers.[11]

Ingrams also suffered in the Blitz:

> Watching the blazing building in the early morning of March 20 1941, Arthur and Geoffrey Ingram felt that all the effort they had put into this new venture, so vital to the war effort, had been wasted. But, by what seemed a miracle, there was no serious hold-up and thanks to the courage of all those working in the offices and factory the work of producing the self-sealing material went on to the end of the war. They knew that their work was a matter of life and death to the allied aircrews.[12]

The Stoke Newington premises of Simpsons, clothing manufacturers whose products supplied the House of Simpson in Piccadilly, took a direct hit on 21 September 1940, resulting in fifty-six casualties, which reduced, but did not entirely incapacitate the production lines. However, the firm acquired premises at Larkhall in Scotland to maintain production and decided to build a new factory there after the war.[13]

ENJOY THE BLACK OUT

Four More Good Reasons for Staying at Home

1. CARLETTE

7/6 PER SET

THRILLING, CAPTIVATING, SENSATIONAL.—The new game that grips and fascinates, appealing irresistibly to all classes and all ages. Any number from two can play this delightful game.

2. MILESTONES

8/6 STANDARD SET.
DE LUXE SETS
12/6 and **21/-**

APPEALS TO EVERYBODY.—The Game of Life. The most interesting and thrilling Family Game ever published. Milestones brings to you the infinite variety of day-to-day happenings which are Milestones on the Journey of Life. All the blending and contrasting phases of an eventful life are intriguingly woven into a wonderful sequence. Milestones takes you through life from the arrival of the Stork to happy and contented retirement.

3. LEXICON

1/- PER PACK
2/6 PER PACK and
5/- TWIN CASE

THE WONDER GAME.—The old favourite for old and young alike. The most interesting, ever-changing, fascinating and amusing card game ever invented.

4. JIG-SAW PUZZLES

9d. and **1/3**

Numerous fascinating designs in Circular Jig-Saw Puzzles ; also the famous Inspector Hornleigh Jig-Saw Puzzles, containing the story of thrilling crime.

May be obtained from all High-Class Stationers and Toy Stores

MANUFACTURED BY

JOHN WADDINGTON LTD.

108, ALBION ROAD, STOKE NEWINGTON, N.16
and at LEEDS *Telephone: Clissold 9171-2-3-4*

Have fun in the blackout. Advertisement for John Waddington Ltd based in Albion Road, Stoke Newington.

The Metal Box Company, based at Urswick Road, not only survived the war but had extended their premises in 1940. The larger premises employed 320 men and women and prided itself on offering full employment, good working conditions, paid holidays and sickness and pension benefit.[14]

Prior to the war, the confectionery manufacturer Clarke, Nickolls and Coombes (registered as Clarnico in 1946) had been the largest of its kind in England. However, production suffered due to the destruction of part of the premises at Hackney Wick but by 1948 the company were looking to reassert their market leadership with the building of large, modern premises from Waterden Road to the canal.[15]

An account survives of the fortunes of Stapley and Smith Ltd, clothing manufacturers based in Sylvester Road:

> One evening in late December 1940, the night skies were torn by bomb blasts and flaming incendiaries. Much of Central London was seared beyond belief and, seemingly, beyond recovery. Prior to that dread night, the great London Wall warehouse of Stapley and Smith had stood firmly as evidence of steady, sterling progress. When morning came only rubble and charred ruination appeared to be left. But there was in fact, very much more remaining. There was the indomitable spirit of the present controllers of the firm.
>
> The spade work of the founders, Sir Richard Stapley and Mr William Smith, was not to go without emulation even in the face of this grievous set back.
>
> In a few short weeks, with everyone concerned refusing to listen to the word 'impossible' Stapley and Smith was able to announce 'Business as usual' to its customers.
>
> The result today is a combination of factory and warehouse staffed by helpers whose happy working outlook is no more clearly evinced than at meal times in the well-kept, well-supplied canteen. All work with a will at the job of making and selling ready to wear garments for ladies and children – the wares proudly displayed at branches all over the country and at the main London showrooms in St Paul's Churchyard.[16]

All the larger factories deployed spotters who kept watch on the roof and fire watchers and factory Home Guards who stayed on the premises overnight. Berger had an effective Home Guard and the Hackney and Stoke Newington Chamber of Commerce arranged through the ARP departments training for people to become factory spotters.[17]

The ARP measures deployed at W.J. Bush, chemical manufacturers, based at Ash Grove off Mare Street, are described in the company's war-time history:

> Rotas for fire watching were drawn up and a squad for each night, consisting of a controller, firemen, first aid and decontamination personnel and spotters, was arranged. The Sports Club House at 56 Ash Grove was equipped with camp beds and blankets, meals being served in the restaurant, and for the first months of the War, night duties were quite pleasant, the evenings being spent at the billiard

A sandbagged roof observation post at the premises of W.J. Bush, Ash Grove.

table and dart board – but not for long – The Blitz in London commenced! From then, life became extremely unsettled. Our sleeping quarters were eventually transferred to the existing club house in Mare Street, these premises being much larger than 56 Ash Grove, but the raids were so numerous and of such long duration, that it became necessary to provide facilities at the assembly point. This assembly point was a portion of a railway arch, and many of us remember the long weary nights spent there during the winter months around the Tortoise stove, where one was roasted on one side and frozen on the other.

To prepare for the anticipated daylight 'blitz' arrangements were made for employees to take shelter in the various basements and underground concrete shelters which had been provided. To each shelter a colour had been allocated and evacuation groups planned. Various trial evacuations had been rehearsed, but it must be said we were not a little worried about what might happen the first time the siren sounded. Our maze of passages and ancient spiral stairways did not appear to accommodate themselves comfortably to the needs of rather excited and rapidly moving crowds of people. But then came the first real evacuation. Evacuation wardens supplemented the official warning with whistles. Nobody fainted, nobody ran, everybody laughed, and quite a number needed powerful persuasion to induce them to go to shelter. Probably most of us expected the

> worst. Thoughts of Guernica were in our minds; but what is the use of thinking, and the best thing to do is to relieve our feelings with a joke and a laugh!
>
> It was not long, however, before it became apparent that many man hours were being lost as a result of continually taking cover. It must be recorded that men working on processes, in the Power House and, let us add, a stalwart who took over the telephone switchboard, remained at their posts – in fact the factory worked throughout the whole war except on two occasions during the night, which is a remarkable tribute to the courage and tenacity, in face of danger, of the average Londoner.
>
> During the winter months the raids started about an hour after blackout and on many occasions we had not finished tea before the fun commenced; raids might last all through the long dark hours of the night, although occasionally there were short periods of 'All clear' to break the continuous alert. The longest raid recorded was of 14 hours duration – from 5.30pm to 7.30am. Our night spotter was in the habit of arriving at 6pm ready to go up on the roof during an alert. . . . From the roof during the raids one could, and generally did, see many thrilling sights such as parachute mines being caught in the searchlights, tracer shells gracefully sliding (so it seemed) towards their target, and sometimes a blinding flash when the mine had been hit in mid-air.
>
> Then there was the second occasion when one of our A.A. shells struck the Power House men's room and exploded, causing a fair amount of damage; only a few minutes previously a stoker had been in the room. Also bombs fell at both ends of Ash Grove as well as at the back of the Works. On another occasion we thought WJB were 'for it' when the gasometer at the end of Ash Grove was hit and set on fire, causing it to burn like an inferno lighting up the whole neighbourhood.[18]

Over two-thirds of the company's pre-war staff went into the armed forces or other civilian work. Replacement personnel had to be trained, while maintaining production levels, and ensuring the defence of the factory. Many of those returning from the armed forces at the end of the war returned to their old jobs. This was a national as well as local phenomenon which forced many of the wartime recruits, often women, back to their former pre-war roles. The prime question then left facing industry was how to ensure that production and business survived against a background of a devastated European market place.

CHAPTER 8

The Home Front on the Path to Victory

The opening of the eastern front in Europe gave the British people, and Londoners in particular, a respite from the almost constant air attack of the previous nine months.

This phase of the war was marked by a number of social dislocations, a shortage of food and consumer goods, the mass recruitment of women into the war effort, the compelling of workers into the Civil Defence movement and armament production and the inadequate provision of education to the nation's children.

Married women, alongside their menfolk, had to participate in compulsory fire watching. All men who worked less than sixty hours a week, and women who worked less than fifty-five hours, had to undertake fire watching, equivalent to one night's duty each week, unless they were already engaged in Civil Defence or Home Guard duties. Fines were levied on those who disobeyed orders:

> Summoned for failing to comply with a direction to report at the wardens' post at Albion Road and for failing to attend for training in fire fighting, Mrs Alice Watts, of 1 Sandbook Road, Stoke Newington, a milk rounds woman, said at North London on Monday that she had to get up at 5.30am. She worked until 4pm and then had to cook her boy's dinner and do the housework. At the time she was directed to attend for training, her husband came home unexpectedly from North Africa on leave, and he wanted her with him all the time, after she finished work.
>
> The magistrate said he recognised that the defendant worked very hard, and it was not easy for her to comply with the direction. He would therefore impose a nominal fine.[1]

Conscription into the armed forces and transfer into essential war manufacture of many thousands of workers meant that many businesses experienced shortages of labour.[2] Local government work was not immune from conscription. A meeting of the Stoke Newington Emergency Committee in November 1941 was called to consider whether

Women of Hackney!

At last an opportunity to help defend your Family, Home, and all that is dear to you—

1st Battalion

Women's Home Defence

Great Inaugural Meeting,

HACKNEY EMPIRE

MARE STREET

Sunday, March 28th—3 p.m.

DOORS OPEN 2-30.

Chairman :

His Worship The Mayor of Hackney

Councillor ALBERT CULLINGTON, J.P.

Miss SIDNEY MALCOLM

Commanding 1st Batt. W.H.D.

AND OTHER WELL-KNOWN SPEAKERS.

GRAND PHYSICAL CULTURE DISPLAY

ADMISSION FREE——————ADMISSION FREE

TRIBE BROS. LTD., Stamford Road, N.1.

Recruitment poster for the 1st Battalion of the Women's Home Defence, 1943.

The grand opening of the St Anne's Day Nursery in Manor Road, Stoke Newington, on 15 November 1941. Joining the Mayor, Councillor Gordon, is Florence Horsbrugh, the Parliamentary Secretary for the Ministry of Health, and the Chairman of the Maternity Committee, Councillor J. Stanton.

the Council should revert to a traditional committee structure, following complaints from councillors not on the Emergency Committee that they were being excluded from the decision making processes of the council. The Emergency Committee argued that:

> all the departments of the Council have been depleted by the calling to the colours of certain of the younger members of the staff and in the early future there will be still further depletion. The resumption of normal meetings would throw considerably increased work on the officers and would entail the engagement of further staff.[3]

The years 1941–4 are marked as years of austerity, shortage and effort. The greatest food shortages were in 1941. German U-boats had successfully reduced the import of food products from overseas. A thriving black market had developed in those goods not subject to rationing or in goods that had been acquired through looting after bomb attack. The *North London Observer* of September 1944 reports one such instance of looting:

> Making his sixth appearance at the North London Police Court on Monday on a charge of stealing a gold wristwatch, three propelling pencils, 569 foreign stamps and four boxes of matches, valued at £11, the property of Nathan Van Veymen from a bombed house at 62 Bethune Road, Stoke Newington, an air raid warden, Gerald James Turner, 54, of Gillam Street, Worcester, who had come to London to help deal with bomb damage was committed for trial at the Old Bailey.
>
> Mrs Hilda Van Veymen stated that when the house was bombed both she and her husband were taken to hospital. Next morning she went to the house with a Mrs Wanky in order to collect some clothing and try to find a handbag containing jewellery. On the way she met the accused, who accompanied her to the house. He did not stay with her all the time, and after a while she called out to him, but could not get any reply, so she proceeded upstairs. She went into the bedroom to look for the handbag and asked the accused to help her, but she could not find it. . . . Corroborating his wife's evidence, Mr Nathan Van Veymen, who appeared in court with his face heavily bandaged, identified as his property all the articles which the police produced as exhibits and said he did not give the accused permission to take any of them. . . .[4]

The prices of goods in short supply soared and profiteers exploited the situation. The *Hackney Gazette* reported:

> War Profiteering by Builders: Stoke Newington Council defrauded . . .
>
> It seems to be a plain case of war profiteering of the very worst sort. You took advantage of the bomb destruction that has gone on in London to make a perfectly illegal profit out of the work of repairing damaged property.
>
> The North London magistrate, Mr W. Blake Odgers, KC, addressed these words on Friday to Henry Thomas Matthews and Thomas Eric Claude Gyles, builders of 120 Lodge Crescent, Waltham Cross who had pleaded guilty to obtaining £11 *6s 6d* on January 2nd, £12 19*s* 5*d* on January 9th and £14 15*s* 7*d* on January 18th from the Stoke Newington Borough Council by false pretences and with intent to defraud. . . . Mr H.A.K. Morgan, counsel for the Director of Public Prosecutions said the two men were in partnership as builders and on December 1st 1940 they got the job of doing first aid repairs for the Stoke Newington Borough Council to bombed premises on the usual terms, the Council paying for wages and materials, plus 15 per cent. . . . As a matter of fact, there was evidence that they had not been working as a carpenter or a slater for the Council at all. They put similar claims in to the Poplar Council.[5]

Black market activity and profiteering in the secondhand clothes market in the Shoreditch and Brick Lane areas are described in Arthur Harding's memoir of his life in Hoxton and Bethnal Green:

The surprising thing about wartime was that the second hand clothes trade, despite the scarcity of coupons, was very brisk. I was buying more suits than I had ever bought before in one day, good quality suits, complete wardrobes. Trade being good I suddenly had enough money to pay my mortgage dues and also the rates. Christmas came and went, and when the children came back home the war was nearly forgotten. I found that people were willing to sell their clothes more readily than before the war, especially those with men who were prisoners of war or missing.

About 1942 I bought a shop at number 250 Brick Lane, and kept it till they served me with an eviction order in 1956. My sister lived upstairs, and downstairs were the old clothes. I still went out to the suburbs, collecting old clothes, shutting up the shop while I was away. Sunday was my best day – same as for the people in the market.

There was a lot of rackets with clothing during the war, and it was through them that I became involved with Scotland Yard's 'ghost squad'. The 'ghost squad' were interested in anything that was detrimental to the war – possessing coupons, or Black Market business. There were people who were making fortunes for themselves out of rationing. Vast quantities of forged coupons were put on the market. In one case they were selling coupons at a shilling a time and when the people who bought them came to undo them, all they found were bits of paper. The crooks in the West End were raiding the town halls to find out where the coupons were stored, and pinching the whole lot. They would sell the coupons at 4*d* or 6*d* each, according to the value of the coupon. The forging was done in the West End – all around Shaftesbury Avenue, but they were sold in the East End. I knew some bleeding villains that was at it.

I knew a lot about the Black Market because of the old clothes business, so I could help the 'ghost squad' a lot. People came in to sell clothing coupons. I used to give £3 a book, but I never sold them for money, only exchanged them for second hand clothes. Mind you I made a great bargain out of it, for £3 I might get £20 of clothing back. I could never understand why wealthy people risked their reputation and character in order to get something the rest of the community wasn't getting. The poorer people used to sell the coupons, because they couldn't afford to buy new clothes, so I exchanged them for old clothing.[6]

Rationing was delayed by the government until January 1940, despite demands to urgently introduce measures to prevent the stock piling of goods by the wealthy who used their cars to buy up an entire shop's stock of sugar. Some shops had already started unofficial rationing to ensure a fairer distribution of goods. Under government rules, each person was entitled to four ounces of bacon and ham, four ounces of butter and eight (increased later to twelve) ounces of sugar each week. By the end of January, the bacon ration had increased to eight ounces a week, an amount which probably exceeded the average weekly intake to the population before the war. Meat rationing followed two months later.[7] Canned and dried goods were brought into the scheme and by July 1942 soap, chocolate and sweets were rationed. The government promoted the 'national wheatmeal loaf', a wholesome but indigestible product which appeared to be universally unpopular with everyone. The white loaf made with scarce, imported, refined flour became an expensive luxury.[8] A cheap milk scheme was introduced by the Ministery of Food in July 1940 for nursing and expectant mothers and children up to the age of five. Surprisingly, bread was not rationed until July 1946.

The boroughs had set up Food Control Committees which monitored population trends, registered rationing mechanisms and ensured that there were enough retail outlets to meet demand. Food distribution points were set up around the three boroughs, either in civic buildings or in borough-run mobile food shops.

Alongside the government control of food rationing, a national Dig for Victory campaign was introduced. This encouraged everyone to grow their own food as a supplement to the goods on ration. Gardens were converted into vegetable plots, and parks, golf courses, sports grounds and other open spaces were dug up. The London County Council allocated land for allotments at Hackney Downs, Hackney Marshes, Millfields, Springfield Park, Victoria Park and Well Street Common and provided training for the growing number of allotment holders as the following letter from W.G. White, the Head of the Junior Commercial and Junior Technical Evening Institute at Millfields School demonstrates:

> Dear Sir,
>
> War Time Food Production in Allotments and Gardens
> Instruction in Gardening
>
> The Council is anxious to help as much as possible in the campaign for increased food production and I am informed that you have recently taken over an allotment in Millfields or Hackney Marsh. I am sure that whatever experience you have in gardening, you would be glad to have the opportunity to increase your skill and knowledge and so obtain the fullest possible benefit from your labour and expenditure. Much disappointment may be avoided by a little timely advice.
>
> I am therefore proposing to open gardening classes here if there is sufficient demand. An expert instructor would be engaged and classes would be arranged on evenings most convenient to the majority of the members. The normal fee would be one shilling and three pence for the term 1st April to 28th June. (This amount may be reduced under certain circumstances.)
>
> Yours faithfully
>
> W.G. White
> Head of Institute[9]

Perhaps Mr White assisted in the scale of agrarian development on Hackney Marshes reported in the *Evening News* in July 1943: 'Harvesting is going on in the heart of London only 4 miles or so from Charing Cross. Within a few minutes walk of Hackney

The public libraries were an important distribution point for food. Here the Stoke Newington Reference Librarians are distributing National Dried Milk.

Left: The customers of F. Fookes, Bakers, of Wick Road in 1942 joining the queue for bread, a staple item not rationed until after the war. Right: Food offices were needed quickly in bomb-damaged areas. This house in Tresham Avenue, Homerton, doubled up as a food office and a fire guard point.

Australian canned food distribution at Hackney Town Hall in 1942.

One of several mobile food shops set up by the Borough of Stoke Newington in 1940.

Town Hall, 33 acres of oats are growing on ground which was once occupied by 17 football pitches. Last year potatoes were grown there. Though a large part of Hackney Marshes is still a playground, and the unenclosed oat fields are near busy roads, not the slightest damage has been done to crops by the public.'

Demand for allotment space was high. At a meeting of Stoke Newington Council in November 1941, it was reported that there were 45 allotment gardens in the borough, controlled by the council and cultivated by local residents. The LCC, the Metropolitan Water Board and private owners had laid out 300 allotments, and there was little remaining land left for cultivation.[10] There were over 1.4 million allotments by 1943. People who lived outside the cities often kept rabbits and chickens. By 1945 Britain was importing only one third of her food requirements compared with two thirds in 1939.

To counteract the shortage of petrol, delivery vehicles and buses carried huge generators containing 'producer' or 'town' gas which fuelled the vehicles. By 1942 over a thousand private cars in Britain were equipped with these strange gas tanks or bags, by which time a ban on petrol for 'pleasure motoring' had been introduced.

Sporting events were curtailed and there were cuts in the clothing ration. But the shortage of clothing workers had meant that not even the clothing ration targets could

Austerity takes hold in 1942. Petrol rationing sees the introduction of tanks of 'producer gas' as a means of fueling buses and cars. (Imperial War Museum, FX 11439D)

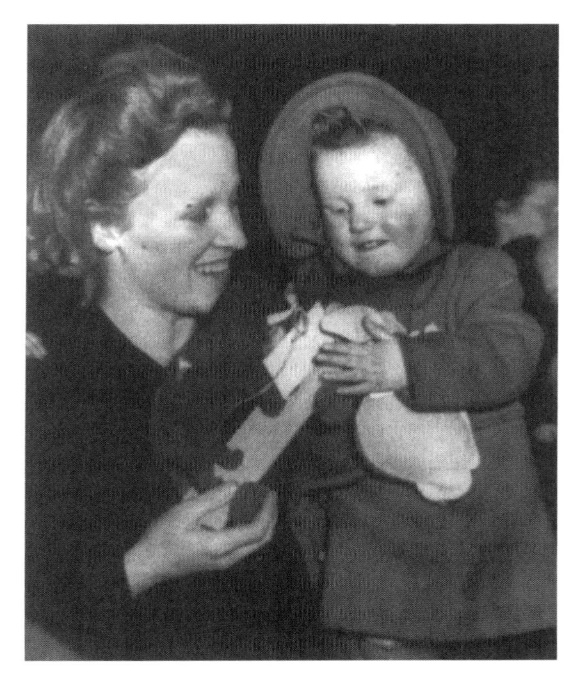

Above left: The Borough of Hackney War Savings Committee standing in front of the sandbagged Town Hall in 1940.

Above right: To combat the national shortage of toys and other goods, Commonwealth countries such as Australia provided Britain with items not given manufacturing priority at home. Here Patricia Dukes of Shoreditch receives a toy from Australia as part of a borough initiative.

Right, above: 'Save Every Scrap'. A salvage exhibition held at Hackney Town Hall, probably in 1943.

Right, below: One of the Borough of Shoreditch 's mobile salvage and recycling trailers seen at the borough's cleansing department at Kingsland Wharf, again probably in 1943.

Left: A decontamination lorry in the parade along Stoke Newington Church Street, War Weapons Week, 17-24 May 1941. Right: A young cub and friend eager to see the latest weaponry on display.

The purpose of War Weapons Week was to raise funds, from the public. Here a woman has her donation recorded. Note the poster in the background: 'Help Stoke Newington to Buy Bombs for Berlin'.

Left: A march past and salute being taken outside Stoke Newington Town Hall.
Right: A section of the parade in Howard Road.

London County Council ambulance staff continuing the public awareness campaign against diphtheria.

be met. As a consequence, the government introduced 'utility clothing' which was controlled in price and quality and designed by top designers. The concept of utility goods spread to other items such as boots, shoes, carpets and furniture.[11]

Austerity measures were largely supported by the British people. The war-time social survey of Britain, *Mass Observation*, makes the point that on many economic issues the people wanted the government to take a hard line on matters which were either felt to he unpopular or issues that the government found politically unpalatable. One survey found widespread support for the nationalisation of the coal industry.[12]

Other campaigns were mounted either by national or local government, such as Save for Victory, Help Build a Plane and Do Not Waste Food. Food waste was separated from household refuse to be fed to livestock, a practice which continued into the 1950s. In tandem with the increase in war production, the first national salvage campaign was launched under the stewardship of Lord Beaverbrook, Minister of Aircraft Production. The *Hackney Gazette* of 15 July 1940 contained a large advertisement for the collection of old iron and other metals which would be collected throughout the borough or could be left at any of the council's depots. A common feature around the three boroughs was the dismantling of the iron railings forming the garden fencing of the Victorian housing stock. The Stoke Newington Borough Council were unenthusiastic when it was first suggested that the Town Hall might set an example to the rest of the local population by allowing the railings around the Town Hall to be taken for scrap iron. They reluctantly consented with the words of Councillor J. Newman Butler, 'I do not think we have any choice in the matter.[13] In the course of the war a reported 18 miles of metal tram track were dismantled in Hackney for salvage.[14]

The 'Help Build a Plane' campaign was vigorously supported in Hackney. Money poured into the Hackney Spitfire Fund with donations coming from all sections of the community – 10*s* from the children of Rushmore Road Infants School, £4 from the tenants of Fawcett House and countless others.[15]

Various other money raising and savings campaigns were started. Stoke Newington held a successful War Weapons Week in May 1941 with the slogan 'Help Stoke Newington to Buy Bombs for Berlin'. The week was well supported with an exhibition in the Assembly Hall where war weapons, models of battleships and aeroplanes were on show. The proceedings took off with a flying start when the Mayor, Councillor J. Newman, took the salute at the Town Hall following a large military parade around the borough.[16]

Other fund raising activities included Warship Week in March 1942. Each of the three boroughs 'adopted' a warship and aimed to raise money for the war effort. Hackney aimed to raise £700,000 for the adoption of the destroyer *Racehorse*, Stoke Newington aimed for £300,00 in support of HMS *Ibis*, a flotilla leader which regrettably was sunk in action in the Mediterranean shortly afterwards. Stoke Newington subsequently 'adopted' the sloop HMS *Mermaid*. Shoreditch sought to raise £500,000 for the submarine *Thrasher*. Part of the Shoreditch campaign involved Lieutenant Roberts, VC, RN, sitting inside a mock-up model of *Thrasher*, which was transported around the Borough. The culmination of Hackney's effort was staged at the Hackney

One of Hackney's fund raising ventures had been the Wings for Victory Week in March 1943. It culminated in a model battleship standing in for the *Bismarck* to the accompanying noise of dive bombers and guns. 'The vessel was sunk by torpedo (in the deep end of the baths) amid joyous acclamation . . .' This event at Clapton Baths was a repeat of the one held a year earlier when a model of the destroyer *Racehorse* had been launched onto the waters of the pool to raise money for Warship Week.

Shoreditch Warship Week in March 1942 saw Lieutenant Roberts VC, RN, paraded around the borough on a mock-up of the submarine HMS *Thrasher* in a bid to raise £500,000.

Central Baths, Lower Clapton Road, when a model of *Racehorse* was floated on the water. The *Gazette* describes the scene:

> The boat with smoke pouring from her funnel, glided majestically along the water, and scores of silver and bronze coins were aimed at her. There were several direct hits, but the Racehorse weathered the showers of metal and yielded a respectable sum for Warship Week. The Mayor announced amid loud applause that the Hackney effort had reached £407,000 that day.[17]

As part of the Warship Week celebrations, a dance was held at St Michael's Hall, Northwold Road. Music was provided by Fred Barnes's Rhythm Boys. The highlight of the evening, however, was the raffle draw when the young female winner was invited to kiss a sailor who had been asked to make the draw. She politely declined but this did not prevent the sailor from taking the initiative by kissing her and taking some minutes to do so.[18]

There was much celebration to mark the 'Salute the Soldier' week in Stoke Newington in November 1944 at a reception attended by Lieutenant General Sir John Brown of the War Office. The people of Stoke Newington had saved and donated over £452,000 against a target of £300,000 for the war effort. Plaques were distributed to the WVS Selling Centre, the Ever Ready Savings Group and to the 9th Battalion County of London Home Guard for their achievements in raising funds for the cause. It was reported that since the beginning of the war, Stoke Newington had saved nearly £4 million channelled through the borough's Saving Committee.[19]

Another significant fund raising activity in Stoke Newington was run by the local Red Cross. Called the 'Penny a Week Fund' its purpose was the provision of parcels to British prisoners of war. Although run as a successful national campaign, there were some seventy active collectors to the fund in Stoke Newington.[20]

The war years saw an increase in demand for books. The *Gazette* highlighted in March 1942 that the demand for reading books from the local community had been 'phenomenal'. As a consequence the Metropolitan Borough of Hackney placed the following advertisement in the *Gazette*:

> To meet the increased demand for books the Borough Council have now opened a temporary branch library at 160 Victoria Park Road. The new branch which is near the junction of Lauriston Road and Victoria Park Road, has a stock of fiction, general works and children's books which may be supplemented by demand by books in any of the other Hackney libraries.
>
> As a relief to war strain books are invaluable: as aids to solving problems which confront the world today books are important: as a means of improving the job you are doing books are a vital necessity. USE YOUR PUBLIC LIBRARIES.[21]

Political life was characterised by campaigns on the Left for the opening up of a second front, a demand soon emerging from the *Daily Express* and *The Times* who supported a growing mood in the country for aid to Russia. A 'Tanks for Russia' week was held

The London Book Recovery and Salvage Drive, June 1943. The Mayor Councillor Albert Lullington, delivers books to an open-air library on the Town Hall forecourt. The borough expected in excess of £350, 000 to be raised. A scrutiny committee examined each book received and divided them into four categories: those of special interest to the armed forces; those felt to be of special value; those needed for re-stocking war damaged libraries; and those to be disposed of.

in September 1941 promoted by Lord Beaverbrook. By the end of the month, aircraft and raw materials were on their way to Archangel. By Christmas German troops were at the outskirts of Moscow but history repeated itself and the invading aggressor was turned back by a combination of the tenacity of the Soviet soldier and the Russian winter.[22]

Support for the Soviet Union came from Hackney. The *Hackney Gazette* of June 1942 made a number of reports on aid and political support:

> THE ANGLO-SOVIET ALLIANCE
> HACKNEY SENDS GREETINGS TO RUSSIA
>
> The first anniversary of the Anglo-Soviet Alliance was celebrated on Friday night by a public meeting attended by representatives of various political, religious and industrial organisations at the Central Hall, Mare Street, Hackney. It had been organised by the Hackney Women's Groups of the Joint Committee for Soviet Aid, which have already done much work in raising money for Soviet medical

> equipment and in sending parcels of knitted garments to the Russian people. On either side of the platform were large photographs of Mr Churchill and Mr Stalin.
>
> The Chair was occupied by the Rev. J.R. Barker, Minister of the Central Hall Mission. . . . The Chairman said they were met to celebrate 12 months of wonderful resistance by the Soviet peoples against our common enemy and the first alliance between Russia and our country, and also the bigger and more recent and far reaching alliance. These augured well for the postwar years and they were pledged to work together with the Soviet Union for the building up of a world order in which the tragedies of the past would not be repeated. He trusted the meeting would pledge themselves to work and strive in support of their brothers and comrades in Russia.
>
> As a result of the collection taken in the hall, which included donations from local trade union branches, factory committees and managements and the money realised on the sale of tickets, a cheque for £80 will be sent to the Joint Committee for Soviet Aid, towards the cost of a mobile X-ray unit for the Red Army. The latter part of the evening was occupied by Unity Theatre, who provided a short sketch entitled 'The Road is Open' and the London Labour Choir who sang a number of Soviet songs.[23]

The event was supported by Sir Austin Hudson, Conservative Member of Parliament for North Hackney, Colonel Loweth, the leader of the Conservatives on Hackney

Sikh troops of the 4th Division marching through Shoreditch on 15 September 1943. (Imperial War Museum, HU 57632)

Council, the Hackney Old Age Pensioners' Association and various industrial organisations.

Links were also forged with the United States. The *Hackney Gazette* reported:

> At 1 o'clock yesterday morning, America heard Hackney workers broadcasting in the special BBC feature entitled 'Bridge Builders'. Four hours earlier a large audience at the Regal Cinema, Mare Street, had watched the recording of this broadcast being made on the stage by six representatives of the borough, including the Mayor, Councillor A. Cullington, JP. The script was written by Mr A.V. Hancock (manager of the cinema) who also produced and presented the whole feature. He had timed it to synchronise with the showing of the film *Yankee Doodle Dandy* starring James Cagney. . . . Four workers from Hackney, Mrs Watson (Austin Reed Ltd), Mr Sid Price (Polikoff Ltd), Mr Robert Bentley (Zinkins Ltd), and Mrs Hornsey (Arthur Cunnington Ltd) then gave their views on America's war effort, and conveyed messages of goodwill to their fellow workers across the Atlantic.[24]

On 7 December 1941 the Japanese had bombed Pearl Harbour and the United States was brought into the conflict, but the elation was short lived as British losses in the Far East and North Africa escalated.

It was not until November 1942 that the tide turned for Britain. The British troops under the command of General Montgomery defeated Rommel and his troops at the battle of El Alamein. This famous victory followed by other successes in North Africa allowed church bells across the land to sound, not as a warning but to herald a change in fortune.[25]

Other successes followed. By 1943 heavy German U-boat losses in the Atlantic forced Admiral Doenitz to recall his fleet which allowed supplies from the United States to Britain to travel unhindered for the next few weeks. Strategic bombing on Germany intensified. The North Africa campaign was concluded and the Allied forces landed on Sicily on 9 July, the start of the invasion of Italy. The Germans were finally repelled on the eastern front in August 1943 at the Battle of Kursk. An ever growing body of people believed that the war would soon be over. There was, however, to be one final onslaught on London before the end was reached, from the flying bombs.

Buzz Bombs

Mrs Barrett, formerly of Sutton Dwellings in Shoreditch recalls her experience of a VI bombing:

Well the thing that actually happened in Shoreditch was the Buzz Bomb, I mean there was loads of blitz's that I was involved in before that, but the thing that happened in Shoreditch as it were was this Buzz Bomb. I was about 13 or 14. When the warning went we used to go in the shelters if we could get there, but on Sundays all the women would have their meat ration, so they defied the buzz bombs as it were to cook Sunday dinner. So when the warning went instead of going straight to the shelters they stayed in their kitchens. Well in our block there's five storeys and four flats on each floor and on one side the balconies, obviously one above the other, and two to the side, so we could sort of hear each other. If we opened the doors we could hear each other. So the arrangement evolved that me on the first floor and Flossie on the fourth floor would stand out there and listen for the buzz bombs, the women would carry on cooking, and then if we heard the buzz bombs coming we would shout 'Buzz Bomb!' or 'Here's one!' and run like mad, and Flossie would bang on the doors on the way down and I would bang on my doors and sometimes we made it, at least we got on to the staircase. You see, you couldn't tell with the buzz bombs. You never knew where they were going to stop but you knew, that when they stopped they glided, sometimes they would just virtually drop, but sometimes they would glide so many yards or half a mile, you just never knew, so you just run like hell when you heard one, so this was the arrangement of a Sunday morning.

Well this particular Sunday morning I had been baking pies with my mother because she was a shelter warden, and she ran the canteen, this was a shelter in Aldersgate Street, Vine Yard it was called. So I was just old enough to, I'd been to school and learned to make these pies, so I used to make these pies for her to sell to the shelters, so we done this, so when the warning went, it was about 12.30, I went to the balcony and I checked with Flossie that she was out there, so anyway we was listening and (of course everybody turned their radio off then) and I just heard two or three chugs in the far distance, and I called out 'Flossie, there's one!' and she 'Well, I didn't hear it'. I said 'Well it is one', so I said 'Come on', and she knew that I was never wrong, I hadn't been wrong so anyway she came out and she banged and she brought everyone down. Well by the time we got to the block entrance you usually heard the thing very close, well of course it was silent then, but I said it would be silent because I heard the cut out. I said 'I know it's coming', and then my father and a couple of the others said 'Oh you're daft, you're just imagining things, it must have been this, that or the other, it would have gone off by now, it would have dropped.' And I said, 'It hasn't, we haven't heard the bang', and I was getting hysterical, I just knew, that the bloody thing was coming; the fact that you don't hear it tells you it's heading for you, you see because all the noise is sort of carried away. So anyway my father and a couple of the others went upstairs again, and I virtually got hold of my mother and dragged her; because the gardens that had been in the grounds were demolished and brick shelters, two brick shelters, had been built there, so they're only virtually a few yards away, a couple of yards. So I dragged my mother over there and all the others thought, let's follow, let's follow for the sake of it. And we just about got to the shelter, when there was this terrible noise; if you can imagine a stick in a gigantic tin can being rattled that's what it sounded like. Of course you knew then that there was one, and we all rushed into the shelter, my mother threw me down on one of the bunks and threw herself on top of me; and then there was this terrible noise like a whip crack that's the only way I can describe it, just like a crack of a whip and you felt this draught come through, and a vibration. But then you wait a few seconds to see if nothing's coming in on top of you, and nothing had come in on top us, and we were still alive so we sort of got up; this was all the people that was in the shelter so we got up and as we came out of the shelter you couldn't see a thing. It was just like the thickest pea-souper that you've ever seen. You virtually couldn't see a hand in front of you, but it was just a pall, a solid pall of dust. And of course everybody thought it was a direct hit on to the blocks we've just come out of, and people were calling out; my mother was calling out for my father, and you know, you could hear people saying 'oh my poor mother', or 'my poor Jack', and this and all screaming out; but you couldn't move, 'cause you didn't know, you couldn't move in case you were falling in debris or whatever. So you just had to stand there and wait for 5 or 10 minutes; you know time stops still at times like that. And then my father came staggering out and he said that he hadn't gone upstairs, he in fact had been talking to two of the people just in the block, well they were very solidly built then, so he was protected from the blast, but of course when we eventually got up to my flat, all the walls were down and falling across the passage, the inner walls were down, all the windows were out, I mean we got all the sticky tape on them, but nevertheless you couldn't cover the whole of the glass, so all that lot was in and all the glass was all over the place, and the doors were blown off their hinges and my mother had got some geraniums out on the balcony, and bits of this was all embedded in the paint work on the balconies and all that was left of the curtains was a fringe, 'cause they were all lace curtains then, they'd been sucked out on to the ruins. However, what has happened, at that time there was a narrow street between our block and another very old block of flats that were terrible slum things and once the people evacuated the landlord and then, I don't know what really happened, but they were empty for some reason or another. Well the buzz bomb had fallen on ruins just behind this block, so this block had taken all the blast and was down, and was sort of lying across this little street so the people that had been in the block were cut by glass and some had been thrown about and hurt their legs, and their arms and other things; but happily nobody was killed.

We did hear that two soldiers had been walking across Petticoat Lane and they would cut across these ruins, Cranwood Street up to East Road and City Road, you see these two soldiers apparently were killed.

But I've got a friend, Eileen, she was about my age and she was running around crying and looking for her parents, and she said her parents, because it was about 1 o'clock now, and she said her parents were due to come back from Petticoat Lane, and she knew instinctively that her parents were under that lot, only nobody was taking any notice of her. They was all dealing with people that was injured and trying to . . . you automatically got a mobile canteen come round with the WVS ladies to give out tea, and the wardens came round to clear away rubble, 'cause the main thing was to get the doors up and the windows, or something up to stop the looters from coming and pinching what bit of home you did have that was left; so anyway, Eileen was crying and got a couple of wardens and she said come and help look for mummy and daddy. I know they'd be coming down this street, and just to please her they started moving some of the bricks, and they found a foot, and it turned out it was her mother's foot, and of course they called the other wardens then and got them out and happily they were still alive, but had Eileen not, you know, carried on like this, they would have been under there for days perhaps and anyway they were got out alive, but of course they were badly cut and they had stitches on their face.[26]

CHAPTER 9

The End and the Beginning

The D-Day landings on the beaches of Normandy commenced on 6 June 1944. Within days, the pilotless planes known as V1s, popularly known as 'Doodle Bugs', reached England. The flying bombs bombarded the south-east by day and by night. It was quickly discovered that if intercepted they would cause as much damage as if they had been allowed to continue their journey unimpeded. Anti-aircraft guns were moved further and further out of London in a bid to bring down these weapons over relatively unpopulated areas. Eventually, the guns were placed on the coast itself. The bombs reigned down during June and July 1944. A fresh evacuation from London occurred, as people fled from weapons that produced an unprecedented number of deaths. By the beginning of August the guns on the coast were becoming adept at intercepting the V1s, about half of them being destroyed before they reached land. By late August Montgomery's eastward advancing army had taken out the V1 launch sites in the Pas de Calais. But the Germans were undeterred. Not only did they continue to launch V1 bombs from aircraft, they unleashed a new and frightening weapon over England, the V2 rocket missile.[1]

The official history of Hackney Downs School details a second round of evacuation of the school to Kings Lynn in Norfolk with the coming of the flying bombs:

> The school at Hackney Downs was under the control of T.B. Barron. A veteran of the Great War, Mr Barron had acted as Mr Balk's right hand man during the first three years of the evacuation. It now fell to him, as acting Headmaster at Hackney Downs, to organise the school during the summer of 1944, when the Germans launched their 'flying bomb' attacks on London. It had previously been decided to close down the school at King's Lynn and to return all Hackney Downs boys and equipment to Hackney for the beginning of the autumn term of 1944. Now these plans had to be abandoned, as many parents understandably sent their sons back to King's Lynn, where these boys, numbering about 140, caused during the last year of evacuation administrative problems easily on a par with those of 1939–1940.

Daubeney Street, 16 July 1944.

Chapman Road, South Hackney, 27 July 1944.

Maury Road, Stoke Newington, 24 August 1944.

The front of the Mare Street Baptist Church, hit on 4 February 1945. The church had already sustained bomb damage in 1940. The site was cleared after the war:

> The building at Hackney Downs suffered badly from blast which, coupled with shrinking numbers, sometime rendered timetables obsolescent. On 23 July 1944, following a 'V2' attack in the vicinity of Amherst Road, all the boys at Hackney Downs were sent home, so that the school broke up on 28 July with no boys at all. When term began again on 5 September the top floor of the school was in ruins and the gymnasium was roofless; the ground floor had been adapted as a Rest Centre, so there were no school lunches. The early months of 1945 were no less hazardous. In January a V2 fell on the Downs and blew out many of the school's windows. Another fell on Sigdon Road in February and blew out more windows. Within a few months, however, nothing remained of the Nazi empire. At the end of the summer term 1945 that portion of the school still in Norfolk bade farewell to Kings Lynn and returned to London.[2]

By early 1945 American strategic bombing of German war installations was accompanied by the blanket bombing of Dresden and other cities, producing fire storms and countless civilian deaths. The Soviet army had reached Berlin, and on 30 April 1945 Hitler was reported to have taken his own life. On 7 May 1945 Germany finally surrendered to the Allied forces at Rheims.

News of the Allied victory was first picked up on German radio on 7 May before any official announcement that the war was over and that the next day would be declared a national holiday. Shops were boarded over, flags and bunting last seen at the coronation in 1937 were brought out, and people took to the streets in tens of thousands.

After his official broadcast to the nation on the afternoon of 8 May, Churchill made his way to Parliament amidst thousands of people. That evening, every public building in London was illuminated as a gesture against six years of the blackout. The day culminated with the appearance of the Prime Minister on the balcony of Buckingham Palace with the King and Queen, the young Princesses, Elizabeth and Margaret, mixing unnoticed with the crowds below. Parties were hurriedly organised and bonfires were lit across the nation as six years of despair, then hope, gave way to euphoria.

VE-Day is described in *The House of Berger 1939–1945*:

> Well, the great day came at least – and what a day! On Monday, May 7th, everyone was on tenterhooks awaiting the official announcement, and we at Berger can at least boast that we were as early with the news as anyone. The internal loud speakers gave news of the German capitulation just after 3 o'clock, and this was followed by a short speech by Mr Harris announcing the holidays, and saying there was nothing left to do but 'Start the rejoicing.' The official news was not issued until later in the evening, but by that time there was victory in the air. Incidentally, on Monday night we were treated to one of the severest thunderstorms for years, accompanied by torrential rain. However, the weather cleared up after this, and was delightful for the whole holiday. As might have been expected, the celebrations proved a huge success, and bonfires were the order of the day.

I should think after the celebrations there was little burnable rubbish left in the whole of England. Just where everyone got the material to burn is hard to say, but get it they did, and a finer collection of fires was never seen. The fires started as a means of excitement for the children, at least that was the story, but once they were started it seemed they formed a full-time occupation for the adults.

Considering the occasion it was all very orderly, and there was not a great deal in the way of refreshments. It is true that nearly everyone had the special bottle that was put away for the great day, but this did not go far and the pubs soon ran dry. Nevertheless, there was enough for everyone to have a little, so we cannot complain. Decorations appeared miraculously on Monday evening, and there certainly seemed no shortage of Union Jacks and hosts of mysterious flags and decorations, saved presumably from the Coronation and Jubilee. In fact it was a great time and everyone seemed to enjoy himself in his own particular way. The feeling of thankfulness and relief was in the air, and I feel a word or two of praise is due to those who arranged the Victory wireless programmes. There was plenty of dance music, marches, speeches, and everything to keep the party going. We all felt that the worst was behind us, realising, of course, that the lads in Burma and the Far East had a nasty business still in front of them. Anyway, we felt certain they would not grudge us a few hours of unrestrained happiness, for we Londoners had also gone through an ordeal that has cost us a great deal in nerves to say the least of the matter. But that is ended, and we can only hope that the powers that be will ensure that such a tragedy is never allowed to happen again. Let us hope

Bunting everywhere in Clapton Passage.

that the years of peace will prove that this struggle has not been in vain, and that this country will really be fit for appreciated heroes and civilians to live in.[3]

Hackney celebrated Victory in Europe in style. The Mayor of Hackney, Alderman Henry W. Butler, attended seventeen victory parties during the Whitsun weekend and made speeches at all of them. These included parties at Sydner Road, Lea View House, Lavender Grove and Navarino Mansions. The party at Roding Road commenced with a tea party for the children and ended with dancing around a bonfire. A recently returned prisoner of war, Lance Corporal Robert Crawford, was the guest of honour at the children's party at Narford Road. He had been captured along with the brother of a local resident at Dieppe and was given a hero's welcome. The entertainment concluded with a Punch and Judy show.[4]

Perhaps the biggest of the local parties was organised by Mr M. Kasler, Deputy Chief Warden, and colleagues from the committee of wardens' post number 6 (based at 79 Cazenove Road) and fellow wardens and fire guards. Attended by 1,500 children, the assembled throng enjoyed a tea, a Punch and Judy show, a

Children of Chelmer Road School, Homerton, standing to attention for a victory photograph.

magician who placed a lady in a box and sawed her in half and music from Alan Kane and his band.[5]

A significant celebration occurred that May when the Princess Elizabeth, on her first solo public engagement, visited the Queen Elizabeth Children's Hospital in Hackney Road. Cheered on by hundreds of well-wishers, the Princess, wearing her ATS uniform, paid tribute to those staff who had kept the hospital running during the German air attacks and pledged her support to the work of the hospital. The event culminated in the Princess announcing that the hospital was to be the recipient of a cheque for £50,000 from an anonymous donor.[6]

Victory in Europe was also a time of contemplation and sorrow. Churches of all denominations were crowded across the three boroughs. The *Gazette* reported on the Victory Service held at St John of Hackney which was attended by local dignitaries and representatives of local wartime organisations.[7] The Alexandra Theatre in Stoke Newington, the area's major venue for boxing matches, was transformed into a temporary place of thanksgiving for a service attended by the Mayor, Councillor Gordon, colleagues, the British Legion, the Stoke Newington Sea Cadets, representatives of the National Fire Service, the Red Cross and others.[8]

In a subdued service, the Mayor attended a thanksgiving service at Brenthouse Synagogue, where the Reverend Melnick paid tribute to all those who had made peace possible, including over one million Jews in the armed services of the Allied nations. Prayers were then said for the millions of Jews murdered in the Nazi gas chambers and labour camps.[9] Hackney's concern for the effects of the Holocaust on the local Jewish community ensured that Thomas Goodrich, Member of Parliament for Hackney Central, was in attendance at the Nuremberg Trials in 1946.

The local Civil Defence and other organisations were officially 'stood down'. A parade followed by a farewell meeting took place at the end of June where the Mayor paid tribute to the contribution made by everyone. Those taking part were reminded of the friendships and spirit of comradeship that had grown during the long years of struggle.[10]

VJ street parties were to he held later in the year, following the cessation of hostilities in the Far East and in commemoration of those who died or suffered imprisonment in the 'Forgotten War'.

Political thinking surrounding post-war reconstruction had first emerged in the aftermath of the Blitz. The government had charged Mr Justice Uthwatt to produce a report concerning post-war planning. Lord Reith, the Minister of Works and Buildings, announced in the House of Lords in July 1941 the government decision to implement the report's recommendations, which included compensation resulting from the public acquisition of land.[11] Social provision in the post-war world was also given due consideration by the National Government.

Following mounting political pressure from the Trades Union Congress in 1941, Arthur Greenwood, the Minister of Health, had commissioned a survey to be undertaken by Sir William Beveridge into all aspects of social insurance provision. His report was published in December 1942 and consisted of three main elements: family allowances for all children, the establishment of a national health service,

The victory salute on the streets of Hoxton. Everyone enjoys a party in Essex Street.

and a national insurance scheme to prevent the excesses of poverty in unemployment, to be backed up by Keynesian interventionist economic principles to reduce mass unemployment. The full report was introduced for debate on the floor of the Commons in February 1943.

Sections of the Conservative Party condemned the Beveridge proposals as inciting laziness. The Labour Party, the Liberal Party, the Church and the population at large applauded the approach, judging by the results of a Gallup Poll which discovered that nine out of ten of those polled supported Beveridge's aims.[12] The government, although adopting the bulk of Beveridge in principle, argued that major policy changes dealing with social insurance should take place only after the election of a new government.[13] Arguably, Churchill's lukewarm stance on Beveridge contributed to the Conservative defeat in 1945. However, the younger elements of the Conservative Party in government, such as R.A. Butler, successfully pushed for change. He pioneered the 1944 Education Act which created a system of secondary education free to all children up to the age of fifteen.

In the aftermath of the publication of the Beveridge Report, debate on the political complexion of a post-war Britain took on fresh momentum. The issues were discussed at a number of public meetings throughout the district. One meeting held by the

Hackney Labour Party in September 1943, addressed by Mr George Ridley, chairman of the Labour Party, conveyed a familiar message:

> Millions of people have noted the characteristics of a world at war – regularity of employment, wages that are better than in the inter-war years, an equitable distribution of essential commodities when they are in short supply, the limitation by taxation of ostentatious and flaunting vulgarity, and the control of an otherwise free, competitive and acquisitive capitalism . . . We live in a world that gives us more food than we can eat, and more clothes than we wear and the workers of the world must see to it that they get a fair deal. We can see the dawning of a new hope – a new belief – for the people of this country after the war.[14]

Sir George Jones, Conservative Member of Parliament for Stoke Newington, addressed the local association in June 1943 on the matter of 'the possibility of a general election in the near future'. He raised the prospect of a continued coalition government charged with the re-building of Britain once the hostilities had ceased. The re-building of the borough after the war had concerned Stoke Newington Borough Council from as early as July 1942. At that time the Emergency Committee had decided that it would be premature to make firm decisions regarding local regeneration in advance of a London-wide plan. One specific concern, however, was the London County Council plan for Woodberry Down.[15] Plans had initially been drawn up for the redevelopment of the site in 1938, but work had not proceeded because of the war. Members of Stoke Newington Council were alarmed when revised plans were brought before them by the London County Council in February 1944. The Housing Sub-Committee reported: 'The main features are 48 blocks of five-storey flats, four blocks of eight-storey flats (all with lifts), and some three-storey dwellings consisting of flats and maisonettes. The total accommodation will amount to 1790 dwellings, containing 5770 rooms.' The London County Council had stated that the eight-storey flats were in the nature of an experiment, and it was hoped that Stoke Newington Council would like them.[16]

According to the *North London Observer* headline which read 'Council motions 8-storey flats – families would be packed like oranges', Stoke Newington Council raised fierce opposition to the scheme. Alderman Miss D.M. Burt in proposing a motion said:

> I cannot reconcile the desire for the ideal post-war planning which is receiving so much publicity, with the apparent desire of the County Council to pack as many people as possible into a small space. There would be no comparison between the 8-storey blocks in the West End and those suggested in Stoke Newington, because the majority of people who could afford to live in the former had country houses and could get away for weekends into the fresh air. The people who unfortunately will be compelled to live week in and week out in buildings little better than barracks, with no privacy and no garden, will not have the opportunity to get away from the surroundings of the flats. This method of living is not conducive to happy family life.[17]

A report by Hackney Town Clerk, Dudley Sorrell, who had maintained this key municipal role throughout the period of the war, showed that the effects of thirty-eight flying bombs dropped on the borough had been devastating. One hundred and thirty fatalities had occurred, 517 serious injuries and 837 less serious injuries. The 38 flying bombs had destroyed 24,300 houses, some hit more than once. Throughout the war, 891 bombs and rockets had fallen on Hackney causing 736 deaths, 2,303 injuries and 200 serious fires. The borough had sought to repair all properties wherever possible, and some 26,000 repairs had been undertaken. Every effort was now to be made to re-glaze all damaged windows.[18] Stoke Newington's statistics, though not as terrible as those of Hackney, showed 204 killed and identified, 6 presumed dead, 10 killed and unidentified, and over 1,100 injured.[19]

The three local councils set to the task of repairing damaged property in order to provide shelter for the homeless and bomb-damaged sites in preparation for the anticipated re-building programme. Prefabricated single-storey homes were hastily erected pending consensus on the London County Council housing plan. They were to provide the homeless, those living in crowded conditions or those from condemned properties with temporary accommodation. Meanwhile, plans were forged for well built and permanent housing to be provided by council direct labour, such as the Forest Road Estate in Dalston which was opened in 1948.[20]

Thoughts now turned to the impending general election. Not surprisingly, there was difficulty in updating the electoral register for the area. The number of voters across Hackney, Shoreditch and Stoke Newington had declined by nearly 40,000 in the years between 1939 and 1945.[21]

The *Gazette* appears to have been in favour of a Conservative victory under Mr Churchill's leadership and favoured the Conservative Party with far more column inches than the other parties contesting the local parliamentary seats. A letter from Mr Churchill to the Conservative candidate for South Hackney, Flight Lieutenant Stanley Price, was disclosed in the *Gazette*:

> On the 3rd September 1939, we began an heroic crusade for Right and Freedom. Our hard task is not yet finished. We have still to beat the Japanese; to work with our Allies to ensure that victory leads to a durable peace; to put this land of ours on its feet again.
>
> Believing that these tasks call for continued national unity, I invited the leaders of the Labour and Opposition Liberal Parties to stay in the Government to help us finish the job. They refused.
>
> Men of goodwill of other parties, and of no party, have accepted the invitation. Together we shall tackle the pressing military and political problems that lie ahead. When those problems have been solved, and Britain is a going concern again, there will be plenty of time to argue about whether we want to discard our whole system of society in favour of strange ideas which are quite out of sympathy with our hard-won individual liberty. Flight Lieutenant Stanley Price is fully pledged to support me. I ask you to give him your vote.[22]

As part of his election campaign, Winston Churchill visited Hackney two days before polling day. 'Big Ovation at Clapton' applauded the *Hackney Gazette*:

> When Mr Winston Churchill visited Hackney on Tuesday night, following his election speech at Walthamstow Stadium, he was given a reception which, if possible, was even more enthusiastic than that of the great cities of the Midlands and the North of England. Only a very small section of the waiting crowd manifested hostility, and its booing and barracking were drowned by overwhelming counter cheers.
>
> For well over an hour before Mr Churchill's arrival, a large crowd had assembled in Cricketfield Road and thoroughfares converging on the Three Sisters public house, opposite which the Prime Minister was to address the gathering. By the time 9 o'clock arrived every point of vantage had been occupied, members of the younger generation even climbing trees to obtain a good view of the proceedings. The steel erection outside the damaged Presbyterian Church was packed with excited youngsters, who scorning danger, held on tenaciously to their precarious perches. Among the crowds there was a fair sprinkling of men and women in Service uniform.
>
> One by one the Conservative candidates arrived. Mr R. Reader Harris (Central Hackney) was the first on the scene, and he received a hearty welcome from many of his supporters. Then other candidates – Captain Sir A. Hudson (North Hackney); Flight Lieutenant S. Price (South Hackney) and Sir George Jones KC (Stoke Newington) – put in an appearance, and all, in turn, were received with cheers.
>
> As this was going on, loudspeaker vans belonging to the Communist and Labour Parties passed to and fro between the lines of the expectant public, and were greeted with ironical cheering.
>
> Promptly at 9.15pm the advertised time, the Prime Minister arrived in a coupe, accompanied by Mrs Churchill. Prolonged cheering and applause followed. Wearing his famous hat and attired in a dark coat and vest, with striped trousers, Mr Churchill was smiling, although looking fatigued. He gave the V sign, and for a time was unable to address the gathering through the small microphone on his car, owing to the tumultuous ovation. When the cheering subsided, and after he had been welcomed by the Conservative candidates, with whom he cordially shook hands, the Premier said:
>
> 'I hope that voting on Thursday will show that the Socialists have not been able to take away the fruits of victory from us. There is no doubt what your duty is. Your country is now at the highest point it has reached in the history of the world, and we can only hold that point by being a strong nation and not falling into foolish errors. Stand together at this critical hour, and I assure you that everything will be done that can be done to re-build the shattered homes of the people and get our trade back. We shall stand with the great nations leading the world into better days.'[23]

But the people of Hackney did not heed the Prime Minister's words. Neither did the people of Britain. They had decided to turn their back on the old order perhaps fearing a return to the unemployment and poverty of the inter-war years.

The *Gazette* of 6 July 1945 reported at the bottom of page one:

> General Election Bombshells – Yesterday's count in connection with the General Election showed that Britain had swung to the Left, and that Labour had achieved some sensational victories. At the time of going to press, the Socialists had secured 379 seats to the Conservatives' 187, and had made no fewer than 205 gains – nearly all of them at the expense of the Tories. . . . Notable Conservative defeats were those of two local MPs, Sir Austin Hudson in North Hackney and Sir George Jones at Stoke Newington. Alderman Herbert Butler, JP goes to St Stephen's as Labour successor to Mr Morrison at South Hackney.
>
> All three of Hackney's new MPs voiced their sentiments at the declaration of the results, and the view of Alderman Goodrich, as the senior Member, speaking from the balcony of the Town Hall, was that 'the people have now made such a turn to the Left as has never before been known. This is a sure sign of the progressiveness of the people, and we promise you now that we will fulfil every pledge that we have made to the last letter.'

In the six years of the post-war Labour government, Labour strove to fulfil many of its pledges, most notably the creation of the National Health Service and the implementation of other recommendations from the Beveridge Report. The railways and the coal industry were taken into public ownership. The measures implemented by the Atlee government became embodied in a postwar consensus that was to last until the late 1970s.

Despite victory in Europe and a new Labour government the privations of war continued into the 1950s and rationing was extended to include bread in 1946. The temporary prefabricated housing built at the end of the war was not so temporary and survived in some areas for decades rather than years. Important buildings such as Hackney Rectory and Brooke House were demolished rather than refurbished. Bomb damaged areas were cleared and gave way to the building of social housing schemes such as St Thomas's Square. Other parts of the three boroughs, which amalgamated in 1963 into the London Borough of Hackney, were cleared for housing schemes not necessarily because of bomb damage, but because sound and architecturally pleasing housing such as Nichols Square in Shoreditch was deemed to be old fashioned. The combination of the Luftwaffe and post-war housing policy had a marked effect on the visual appearance and the social character of housing in Hackney.

However, of greater importance to many local people was the fact their lives would never be the same again. The loss of loved ones serving overseas, the loss of men, women and children in the death camps and the loss of life in the bombing raids over the three boroughs represent personal, political and moral tragedies which must not be forgotten. Neither must they be allowed to happen again.

Studying the Second World War in Hackney

The following bodies hold records and artefacts that will help with the study of the Second World War in Hackney.

London Borough of Hackney, Hackney Archives, 43 De Beauvoir Road, London, N1 5SQ. Tel: 020 7241 2886. Email: archives@hackney.gov.uk. www.hackney.gov.uk/ca-archives.

Hackney Archives holds the records of Hackney Council and its predecessor authorities (Hackney, Shoreditch and Stoke Newington Metropolitan Boroughs), whose officers participated in ARP services during the war, together with committee and departmental records. These include bomb damage maps for Hackney and Stoke Newington, incident files, and the extensive photographic record of significant bomb incidents commissioned by Hackney. Individual family papers include rationing material and other papers; especially useful is the collection of ARP diaries of T.E. Browne who served in Hackney. Some of the lists of archives held can be found on the Access to Archives database at http://www.nationalarchives.gov.uk/a2a and on Hackney Archives' own online catalogue, which is constantly being updated and is available at http://www.hackney.gov.uk/ca-archives-webcat.

Hackney Archives also has a local studies library, which includes some written and oral history reminiscences. The visual collection contains photographs of victory celebrations and there is a short film of an official military victory parade as it passed Bethnal Green Town Hall in 1946.

Hackney Archives is currently open to the public (no appointment necessary) Tuesday–Friday (times vary). For the latest opening hours, please check the website at http://www.hackney.gov.uk/ca-archives or telephone the Archives.

London Borough of Hackney, Hackney Museum, Technology and Learning Centre, 1 Readling Lane, London, E8 1GQ. Tel: 020 8356 3500. Email: hmuseum@hackney.gov.uk. www.hackney.gov.uk/hackneymuseum.

Hackney Museum presents the history of the borough in an attractive, thematic, way. It includes a special section on the Second World War with a reconstructed bomb shelter, and displays of ARP uniform and equipment, excerpts from the diary of Clapton Warden Mr T.E. Browne, and war-time posters and photographs.

Primary school groups can book a special visit that includes a special object-handling workshop to explore life in Hackney during the war and the experiences of evacuees.

The Museum also offers a wide range of events and activities for both families and adults, some of which cover the war-time period. For current programmes check the website or contact the Museum.

The museum is free to visit, and the opening times are:

Monday: Closed. Tuesday: 9.30am–5.30pm. Wednesday: 9.30am–5.30pm. Thursday: 9.30am–8pm. Friday: 9.30am–5.30pm. Saturday: 10am–5pm. Sunday and Bank Holidays: Closed.

Civil Defence bunker, 22 Rossendale Street, E5.

Includes original room layout and air handling plant. Open by volunteers. Details advertised in local papers.

Geffrye Museum, 136 Kingsland Road, London, E2 8EA. Tel: 020 7739 9893. Email: info@geffrye-museum.org.uk. www.geffrye-museum.org.uk.

The Geffrye Museum depicts the quintessential style of English middle-class living rooms. Its collections of furniture, textiles, paintings and decorative arts are displayed in a series of period rooms from 1600 to the present day. There is also a library and archive, which includes furniture trade catalogues.

The museum is open Tuesdays to Saturdays 10 a.m. to 5 p.m. and on Sundays and Bank Holiday Mondays 12 to 5 p.m. The archive is available by prior appointment with museum staff.

London Metropolitan Archives, 40 Northampton Road, London, EC1R 0HB. Tel: 020 7332 3820. Email: ask.lma@cityoflondon.gov.uk. www.lma.gov.uk.

The LMA holds the records of London County Council, including the fire brigade. The LCC played a major role in co-ordinating services in London during the Second World War and the LMA has substantial holdings of committee minutes and departmental papers. The collections include war damage maps for the LCC area and the record made of the council's part in evacuation.

A publication about the LCC's part in evacuation, *We Think You Ought To Go,* is available from LMA price £5 while stocks remain.

The London bomb damage maps were published by the London Topographical Society in 2005: *The London County Council bomb damage maps, 1939–1945*, introduction by Robin Woolven, edited by Ann Saunders, 2005. This publication is now unfortunately out of print.

The LMA is open Tuesdays 9.30 a.m. to 7 p.m. and Wednesdays to Fridays 9.30 a.m. to 4.45 p.m.

Museum of London, London Wall, London, EC2Y 5HN. Tel: 020 7001 9844. Email: info@museumoflondon.org.uk. www.museumoflondon.org.uk.

Displays and artefacts. Written reminiscences of Londoners are held in the library and can be consulted by prior appointment.

Air Raid Precaution Centre, 24 Rossendale Street

The bunker was built to co-ordinate North Hackney's Second World War anti-air raid offensive and has been awarded grade II listed building status. The Centre was commemorated by a Hackney brown plaque on 25 April 1994. For more information, see the information about Hackney's brown plaques on the Hackney Council website at http://www.hackney.gov.uk.

Buildings and Memorials of the Second World War in Hackney

Hackney's main ARP offices were at 219-231 Mare Street and still survive. The Rossendale bunker is listed above. War memorials were put up at St John at Hackney and in the grounds of Hackney Town Hall. This simple cross has recently been moved to the front of the Town Hall forecourt. Stoke Newington acquired a hall in Clissold Road to display a book of remembrance and laid the forecourt out as a garden.

There are many other memorial plaques in local churches, schools and other premises. The Imperial War Museum is undertaking a survey of surviving war memorials and would be interested to hear from anyone who knows of any locations not usually open to the general public.

Notes

Chapter 1

1. Labour Party and the Tailor and Garment Workers' Union 1937-1940, HAD D/S/24/4/131; David Thomson, *England in the Twentieth Century (1914–1963),* Penguin, 1965
2. *Hackney Gazette*, July *22* 1938
3. David Mander and Jenny Golden, *The London Borough of Hackney in Old Photographs (1890–1960),* Alan Sutton, 1991
4. Ibid
5. *Hackney Gazette,* August 29 1938
6. *North London Recorder*, Special Odeon Supplement, July 27 1938
7. *Hackney Gazette,* May 3 1939
8. David Thomson, *England in the Twentieth Century (1914–1963),* Penguin, 1965

Chapter 2

1. A.J.P. Taylor, *English History (1914–1945),* Oxford University Press, 1965
2. Ibid
3. Ibid
4. Ibid
5. Ibid
6. *Hackney Gazette*, May 31 1937
7. Phil Piratin MP, *Our Flag Stays Red*, Thames Publications, 1948
8. Cuttings on Oswald Mosley and Hackney 1937, HAD H\LD\7\51
9. *Hackney Gazette*, March 1 1939
10. *Hackney Gazette*, March 13 1939
11. Morris Beckman, *The 43 Group*, Centerprise, 1992
12. Papers of Albert Cullington, HAD D\F\CUL
13. Correspondence between the Jewish Peoples' Council, the Labour Party and the Tailor and Garment Workers' Union 1937-1940, HAD D/S/24/4/13
14. Workers' Circle Friendly Society Records 1909–1984, HAD D/S/61
15. Morris Beckman, *The 43 Group*, Centreprise ,1992
16 Ibid

Chapter 3

1. HAD H/G/15 and SN/S/4
2. HAD
3. HAD SN/G/10
4. Ibid
5. HAD H/G/16
6. HAD H/G/17
7. HADH/A/1
8. *Hackney Gazette*, July 29 1938
9. Department of National Heritage, 735/10009 1993
10. *Hackney Gazette*, June 27 1938
11. *Hackney Gazette*, March 23 1938
12. *Daily Telegraph*, June 27 1938
13. *Hackney Gazette*, July 6 1938
14. *The Star*, September 3 1938
15. *Hackney Gazette*, September 30 1938
16. *Hackney Gazette*, October 21 1938
17. *The Recorder*, October 7 1938
18. HAD
19. HAD
20. J.B.S. Haldane, *A.R.P.*, Left Book Club (Victor Gollancz), 1938
21. *Hackney Gazette*, January 30 1939
22. *Hackney Gazette*, May 12 1939
23. *Hackney Gazette*, September 1 1939
24. *The Recorder*, April 29 1939
25. *Hackney Gazette*, August 28 1939
26. *The Outlook*, Evacuation Edition, North Hackney Central School at Buntingford Senior School, Hertfordshire, Christmas 1939.

Chapter 4

1. Angus Calder, *The People's War*, Pimlico, 1969
2. Ibid
3. Papers of F.H. White, HAD D\F\WHI\2
4. *Hackney Gazette*, September 13 1939
5. 'Goodbye Home'. Oral history transcript by Constance Charlton, HAD
6. *The History of Hackney Downs School*, HAD
7. Stoke Newington ARP, News and Notions of Civil Defence, HAD
8. *The Outlook*, North Hackney School Magazine, Christmas 1940
9. Angus Calder, *The Peoples' War*, Pimlico 1969
10. *Hackney Gazette*, July 15 1940
11. *Hansard*, June 6 1940
12. A.J.P. Taylor, *English History (1914–1945)*, Oxford University Press, 1965
13. Leaflet of a speech by Adolf Hitler to the Reichstag, dropped by plane over London, July 1940, HAD Y3551
14. HAD SN/A/38
15. Angus Calder, *The Peoples's War*, Pimlico, 1969
16. Ibid

Chapter 5

1. Miller and Bloch, *Black Saturday: The First Day of the Blitz*, HAD Y5194
2. *Front Line 1940–41: The Official Story of the Civil Defence of Britain,* HHMSO, 1942
3. Angus Calder, *The Peoples's War*, Pimlico, 1969
4. H.A. Wilson, *Death Over Haggerston*, A.R. Mowbray & Co., 1941
5. *Hackney Gazette*, September 27 1940
6. *Hackney Gazette*, September 25 1940
7. *Hackney Gazette*, October 21 1940
8. *The Outlook*, North Hackney School Magazine, Christmas 1940
9. Ibid
10 Oral history transcript by Cecil Alexander Sindell, HAD
11. *Hackney Gazette*, April 23 1941
12. *Front Line 1940–41: The Official Story of the Civil Defence of Britain*, HMSO, 1942
13. T.E. Browne, *War Diaries and Papers*, HAD D\F\BRO

Chapter 6

1. *Front Line 1940–41: The Official Story of the Civil Defence of Britain*, HMSO 1942
2. Ibid
3. Shoreditch ARP Control Message Records, HAD
4. Stoke Newington ARP, News and Notions of Civil Defence, HAD
5. *The Outlook*, North Hackney School Magazine, Summer 1942
6. Ibid
7. Angus Calder, *The Peoples' War*, Pimlico, 1969
8. HAD H/CC/2/20
9. *North London Observer*, August 14 1943
10. Oral history transcript by Florence Davy, HAD

Chapter 7

1. David Thomson, *England in the Twentieth Century (1914–1963)*, Penguin, 1965
2. Angus Calder, *The Peoples' War*, Pimlico, 1969
3. *Hackney Gazette*, April 20 1942
4. Angus Calder, *The Peoples' War*, Pimlico, 1969
5. Ibid
6. *Furnishing the World*, the East London Furniture Trade 1830–1980
7. *The History of R & J Hill*, HAD, 1942
8. Hackney Annual Report, 1948
9. HAD D/B/BER/2/7/48
10. Ibid
11. *A History of Progress and Development*, HAD, J.G. Ingrams & Son Ltd
12. Ibid
13. Hackney Annual Report, 1948
14. Ibid
15. Ibid
16. Ibid
17. *Hackney Gazette*, August 8 1941
18. *W.J. Bush at War 1939–1945*, HAD

Chapter 8

1. *North London Observer*, November 27 1943
2. Angus Calder, *The Peoples's War*, Pimlico, 1969
3. *Hackney Gazette*, November 28 1941
4. *Hackney Gazette*, September 29 1944
5. *Hackney Gazette*, October 20 1941
6. Raphael Samuel, *East End Underworld: Chapters in the Life of Arthur Harding*, Routledge & Kegan Paul, 1981
7. Angus Calder, *The Peoples' War*, Pimlico, 1969
8. Ibid
9. Papers of F.H. White, HAD D\F\WHI\2
10. *Hackney Gazette*, December 1 1941
11. Angus Calder, *The Peoples' War*, Pimlico, 1969
12. Ibid
13. Ibid
14. Hackney Annual Report, 1948
15. *Hackney Gazette*, October 30 1940
16. *Hackney Gazette*, May 5 1941
17. *Hackney Gazette*, March 27 1942
18. Ibid
19. *Hackney Gazette*, November 20 1944
20. *Hackney Gazette*, July 29 1942
21. *Hackney Gazette*, March 2 1942
22. Angus Calder, *The Peoples' War*, Pimlico, 1969
23. *Hackney Gazette*, June 22 1942
24. *Hackney Gazette*, April 30 1943
25. Angus Calder, *The Peoples' War*, Pimlico, 1969
26. Oral history transcript by Mrs Barrett, HAD

Chapter 9

1. Angus Calder, *The Peoples' War*, Pimlico, 1969

2. *The History of Hackney Downs School*, HAD
3. HAD D/B/BER/2/7/48
4. *Hackney Gazette*, May 25 1945
5. *Hackney Gazette*, May 30 1945
6. *Hackney Gazette*, May 28 1945
7. *Hackney Gazette*, May 16 1945
8. *North London Observer*, May 19 1945
9. *Hackney Gazette*, May 19 1945
10. *Hackney Gazette*, July 4 1945
11. *The Times*, July 18 1941
12. British Institute of Public Opinion, *The Beveridge Report and the Public*, 1943
13. Angus Calder, *The Peoples' War*, Pimlico, 1969
14. *Hackney Gazette*, September 27 1943
15. *Hackney Gazette*, July 31 1942
16. *Hackney* Gazette, February 28 1944
17. *North London Observer*, March 4 1944
18. *Hackney Gazette*, October 4 1945
19. Metropolitan Borough of Stoke Newington War Record, July 16 1945, HAD SN\A\3
20. Hackney Annual Report, 1948
21. *Evening Standard*, May 24 1945
22. *Hackney Gazette*, July 4 1945
23. *Hackney Gazette*, July 11 1945

Bomb Incidents

This list is compiled from three lists prepared by council officers and based on air raid precaution records. No complete record of bomb incidents survives for Shoreditch, which chose instead to keep a record of damage to all property, but not what caused it. Only entries for the Hoxton area survive.

AB	anti-aircraft shell	OB	oil bomb
BB	barrage balloon	PM	para mine
DA	delayed action	RS	rocket shell
GB	gas bomb	SB	suspect bomb
HE	high explosive	UXAA	unexploed AA shell
I	incendiary	UXB	unexploded bomb
LM	land mine	UXM	unexploded mine
M	mine	V1	
MOL	Molotov	V2	
NB	not bomb		

Hackney

1940

Sunday 25 August

Bartrip Street	HE
Forest Road, No. 80	SB
Mallard Street	UXB
Weston Street, Bethnal Green	HE

Saturday 7 September

Andrews Road	HE
Beaumont Court, Lower Clapton Road	HE
Brookc Road & Maury Road	HE
Buckingham Road, No. 57	UXB
Conrad Street, No. 10	I
Cresset Road	UXB
Durham Grove, London Fields, East Side No. 24	HE
Ellingfort Road	HE
German Hospital	HE
Glenarm Road	HE
Hackney Marshes	I
Hackney Police Station	UXB
Helmsley Terrace	HE
Kenninghall Road	HE
King Edward's Road, No. 92	I
Lamb Lane	HE
Lauriston Road	HE
London Fields Station, Railway Track	HE
London Lane	HE
Lower Clapton Road	HE
Lower Clapton Road, No. 235	
Lower Clapton Road	HE
Mare Street	UXB
Mare Street, Lyme Grove & Brenthouse Road	HE
Median Road, No. 23	UXB
Mentmore Terrace	HE
Midhurst Road	UXB
Milbourne Street	UXB

Osborne Road	UXB
Percy Terrace	UXB
Prince Edward Road	HE
St Thomas's Square	HE
Templecombe Road	HE
Valentine Road	HE
Well Street, LPTB Garage	DA

Sunday 8 September

Ballance Road, No. 33	
Berger's Factory, Morning Lane	I
Berkshire Road	
Bower Road	
Brooke House	UXB
Brooke Road, No. 101, & Norcott Road, No. 17	UXB
Chatham Place	HE
Chevet Street	I
Colveston Crescent, No. 52	UXB
Cricketfield Road	HE
Dalston Lane, No. 30	HE
Gore Road & St Agnes Terrace	HE
Graham Road, Near Railway, No. 217	UXB
Hackney Churchyard	I
Halidon Street	HE/DA
Hollar Road	HE
Homerton High Street	HE
Kenninghall Road, The Retreat	HE
Kenninghall Road, No. 32	HE
King Edward's Road	UXB
Lesbia Road & Median Road	UXB
Lower Clapton Road, Pond Shelter	
Lyme Grove	HE
Mayfield Road	HE
Middleton Road Bridge	HE
Middleton Road, No. 49	I
Norcott Road, No. 29	UXB
Nightingale Road	
Queensdown Road	HE
Queensdown Road, No. 29	HE
Richmond Road, Petrol Station	I
Tudor Grove, No. 21	
Victoria Park, Wallis Road	HE
Wallis Road & White Post Lane	HE

Monday 9 September

Benyon Road, No. 26	NB
Bodney Road	OB
Bodney Road	UXB
Casterton Street, Railway at rear	UXB
Clarence Road & Rowhill Road	HE
Cleveleys Road	HE
Cotesbach Road, Lea Bridge Road	
Dalston Station	
Downham Road & Southgate Road	HE
Downs Road, No. 71	HE
Ferncliffe Road	HE
Gomer Terrace & Prout Road	HE
Gunton Road, No. 40	UXB
Hackney Marshes, near Dressing Rooms	UXB
Homerton High Street, No. 98	HE
Isabella Road, No. 4	NB
Kingsland Road, No. 534	HE
Loddiges Road, No. 57	UXB
Mountford Road	
Queensdown Road, No. 13/15	HE
Southgate Road, No. 13/14	HE
Upper Clapton Road	
Victoria Park, near Running Track	UXB

Tuesday 10 September

Kingsland Road, No. 318	I
Milbourne Street	UXB

Wednesday 11 September

Portland Avenue, No. 22	AA
Stamford Hill, No. 111	HE

Thursday 12 September

Bergholt Crescent	I

Friday 13 September

German Hospital	I
Thornby Road	

Monday 16 September

Ballance Road	I
Ballance Road & Kenworthy Road	DA
Bentham Road, No. 111	NB

Bradstock Road & Cassland Road	I
Cadogan Terrace Trenches	
Cassland Road	HE
Cassland Road & Terrace Road	I
Cazenove Road, near Alkham Road	I
Cranwich Road & Dunsmure Road	I
Darnley Road	I
Digby Road	HE
Dunsmure Road, No. 92	I
Eleanor Road	AA
Gascoyne Road	OB
Kenworthy Road	NB
Mare Street, Lansdowne Club	DA/HE
Metropolitan Hospital	BB
Mount Pleasant Lane School	AA
Oval, Mare Street	I/HE/OB
Tresham Avenue	HE
Victoria Park Road, No. 214	AA
Victoria Park, Running Track	HE
Victoria Park Road, near Shore Road	HE
Weald Square	UXB
Wick Road, No. 150	HE
Wick Road, No. 168	I
Wick Road, Post Office	I

Tuesday 17 September

Amhurst Road, near Sydner Road	HE
Bentley Road, No. 11	I
Blurton Road	HE
Cadogan Terrace	HE
Dunlace Road, No. 29	HE
Eastway, LMS Coalyard	HE
Elderfield Road, No. 178	HE
Electricity Works	NB
Hackney Marshes, Pond Lane Bridge	AA
Halidon Street, No. 49	HE
Homer Road	HE
Lockhurst Street	HE
Millfields Road, near Glyn Road	HE
Powerscroft Road	HE
Radley Square, Nos. 9/10	AA
Upper Clapton Road, near Northwold Road	BB
Urswick Road, Upton House School	HE
Victoria Park Station, Signal Box	HE

Wednesday 18 September

Alcester Crescent & Comberton Road	HE
Amhurst Park, No. 26	AA
Arcola Street, No. 40	HE
Ballance Road	HE
Balls Pond Road, near Burder Road	HE
Bayston Road, Nos. 71/73	UXB
Bayston Road	HE
Benthal Road, No. 56	HE
Bentham Road, No. 145	NB
Blanchard Road, No. 16	
Chatsworth Road & Mildenhall Road	HE
Culford Road	I/OB
Darville Road	HE
Daubeney Road, No. 198	HE
Eastway	I
Elderfield Road/Glyn Road, No. 265	HE
Ellingfort Road & Mare Street	HE
Evering Road, No. 188	AA
Farleigh Road	HE/OB
Florfield Road, No. 4	AA
Fortescue Avenue & Mare Street	HE
Hackney Marshes, Eastway & Homerton Road	UXB
Hassett Road	HE
Hindle House, Shacklewell Row	HE/I
Kingsland Road, No. 405	I
Kingsland Road, No. 443	HE
Lenthall Road, No. 56	HE
Maclaren Street	HE
Mare Street, Lady Holies School	HE
Mare Street, Regal Cinema	UXB
Mount Pleasant Hill, Lathams Timber Yard	I
Overbury Street	HE
Rushmore Road, Nos. 222/226	HE
Simpsons Factory, Somerford Grove	HE
Southwold Road	HE
Stamford Hill, No. 122	
Stamford Hill, Clarks College	AA
Stoke Newington High Street, opp. Police Stn	HE
Sydner Road, Nos. 45/46	HE
Tyssen Road	HE

Wick Road, Barnabas Road, Hedgers Grove HE
Wick Road, No. 164

Thursday 19 September

Bannister House HE
Barnabas Road, No. 26 I
Castlewood Road HE
Craven Park School HE
Dunsmure Road, No. 81 AA
Dunsmure Road, No. 92 HE
Elderfield Road, near Rushmore Road HE/I
Elderfield Road
Farleigh Place DA
Gunton Road, No. 30 HE
Leadale Road, Nos. 63/67 HE
Linthorpe Road, No. 34 UXB
Lower Clapton Road, Nos. 103/105 HE
Mare Street, Horse & Groom UXB
Olinda Street HE
Powerscroft Road, Nos. 59/61 HE
Powerscroft Road HE
Stamford Hill, near Windus Road I
Stamford Hill, near Clapton Common HE
Thornby Road, No. 49 HE
Timber Wharf Road HE
Wensdale House, Upper Clapton Road HE
West Bank, No. 39 UXB
West Hackney Church HE

Friday 20 September

Ainsworth Road HE
Benthal Road School HE
Brooke Road, No. 122 AA
Brougham Road, No. 40 HE
East Bank, No. 30 AA
Evering Road HE
Evering Road & Benthal Road I
Hackney Marshes, Wooden Bridge UXB
Hindle House AA
Horne Brothers, Tudor Road HE
Kingsland Road, No. 322 AA
Mare Street, Gerrish Ames & Simkins HE
Oldhill Street, Nos. 3–7 HE
Rectory Road, No. 13a UXB
Sanford Lane HE
Shacklewell Lane, Green Man AA
Shore Road & Well Street, Johnsons Factory HE
Sydner Road AA
Westgate Street OB

Saturday 21 September

Amhurst Road, North London Club
Amhurst Road NB
Cazenove Road, No. 84 I/OB
Comberton Road, No. 9 UXB
Downham Road AA
Eleanor Road & Richmond Road HE
Eleanor Road School HE
Filey Avenue & Osbaldeston Road I/OB
Gore Road LM/UXB
Kingsland Road HE/AA
London Fields, Centre Path HE
Navarino Mansions AA
Simpsons Factory, Somerford Grove HE

Sunday 22 September

Ballance Road I
Ballance Road, Presbytery I
Bayford Street HE
Benn Street, Nos. 24/25 I
Cassland Road Church I
Cassland Road & Harrowgate Road I
Cawley Road Trenches I
Conner Road, Marshall & Co. I
Eleanor Road, between Wilton Way & Richmond Road HE
Gascoyne Road DA
Groombridge Road, No. 30
Hassett Road, No. 78
King Edward's Road HE
Navarino Mansions HE
Oakfield Road AA
Retreat Place I
Well Street, between Poole Road & Kenton Road I
Wetherall Road, UD Depot (United Dairies) I

Wetherall Road, Royal Hotel I
Wick Road, No. 260a I
Wilton Way, between Navarino Road & Royal Oak Road HE

Monday 23 September

Adley Street & Ashenden Street, No. 86 I
Amhurst Park, No. 42 HE
Amhurst Park, Nos. 66/68 HE
Bentham Road & Harrowgate Road I
Bethune Road & Dunsmure Road HE
Clarnico's (Hackney Wick) HE
Denver Road & Durley Road HE
Foulden Road, Nos. 80/82 HE
Hillside Road, Hurstdene Gardens HE
Lee Conservancy Road HE
Olinda Road HE
Ravensdale Road, No. 34 HE
Retreat Place, No. 37 I
Sherry's Timber Wharf I
Stamford Hill, No. 153 HE

Tuesday 24 September

Amhurst Road, No. 114 AA
Amhurst Road, between Marcon Place & Spurstow Road HE
Ballance Road Church I
Benthal Road, Nos. 2/10
Blurton Road HE
Bodney Road HE
Britania, Mare Street HE
Cawley Road Trenches HE
Chelmer Road HE
Downs Park Road, Lungleys HE
Downs Park Road, No. 22 AA
Evering Road I
Glaskin Mews HE
Glyn Road & Presburg Street HE
Hackney Downs, Railway Station UXB
Heatherley Road AA
Hertford Road, No. 141 AA
Kenninghall Road
Landfield Street HE
Lea Navigation Cut HE
Oakfield Road I
Rockmead Road HE
Shacklewell Lane, No. 24 HE
Shacklewell Lane, The Baths HE
Sigdon Road School HE
Victoria Park Road, No. 251 DA

Wednesday 25 September

Clapton Stadium DA
Clarence Road & Rowhill Road HE
Clifden Road, No. 104 UXB
De Beauvoir Square HE
Downham Road OB
Englefield Road Baths HE
Enfield Road School HE
Hertford Road, No. 103 HE
Lamb Lane HE
Mare Street, Zinkins Factory DA
Mare Street, Police Section House HE
Morris's Timber Wharf UXB
Stamford Hill, Nos. 107/9 LM
Tottenham Road, No. 45 HE
Tudor Road, No. 25 DA
Tottenham Square HE

Thursday 26 September

Blackstone Road, Nos. 31/39 I
Brenthouse Road HE
Cresset Road HE
Dalston Lane, No. 69 UXB
Dynevor Road, Tyssen Road, Manse Road, No. 28 LM
Eleanor Road I
German Hospital UXB
Harrowgate Road, No. 22 UXAA
London Fields, near Eleanor Road UXB
Navarino Road OB
Sherry's Timber Wharf I
Wilton Way, near Navarino Road I
Wattisfield Road, Disabled Soldiers' Home UXAA

Friday 27 September

Colverstone Crescent & Ridley Road I
Downham Road, Wardens Post AA
LMS Railway, near Dalston Junction HE
Odeon Cinema, Kingsland Road HE
Perch Street, No. 22 I

St Marks Rise, Saville Piano Company I
Shacklewell Lane I
Stoke Newington Road, No. 10 I
Tottenham Road, Nos. 36/40 HE

Saturday 28 September
Amhurst Road, No. 329 I
Englefield Road Baths HE
Englefield Road, Nos. 4/10 HE
Hertford Road HE
Kingsland Road HE
South Hackney Churchyard AA

Sunday 29 September
Comberton Road, No. 22 I

Monday 30 September
Banbury House, Wetherall Road AA
Mabley Green, Shelters NB
Sach Road OB

Tuesday 1 October
Windus Road, Wheatsheaf Public House HE

Thursday 3 October
John Campbell Road, No, 26 AA
Victoria Park, Hard Tennis Courts AA

Friday 4 October
Eastway, Hackney Marshes UXB
Ritson Road AA

Saturday 5 October
Clapton Common, between Rookwood Road & Stamford Hill
Firsby Road I
Hillsea Street, Nos. 19/21 HE/I
Leweston Place, No. 24 I
Ottaway Street, Nos. 30/40 HE
Portland Avenue I
Rectory Road HE

Monday 7 October
Brooksbank Street & Well Street HE
Cazenove Road HE
Chalgrove Road HE
Homerton Terrace & Retreat Place HE
Kenninghall Road, No. 57
Kyverdale Road, No. 58 HE
Northwold Road, Stapleton's Diary OB
Poole Road HE
Well Street Common Trenches HE

Tuesday 8 October
Bay Street HE
Cassland Road/Queen Anne Road HE
Chatham Place & Morning Lane HE
Dalston Lane, Nos. 255/257 AA
Garnham Street OB
Glading Terrace, No. 10 OB
Mapledene Road HE
Meynell Road HE
Middleton Road HE
Miller's Coal Wharf; Hackney Station HE
Osbaldeston Road, No. 57 UXB
Poole Road, No. 22 HE
Rockwood Road HE
Valentine Road HE
Well Street, between Cresset Road & Collent Street HE
Well Street Common, Sandpit UXB

Wednesday 9 October
Dunsmure Road, No. 18 HE
Gayhurst Road, No. 39 HE
Mabley Green HE
Mapledene Road HE
Mapledene Road & Lansdowne Drive HE
Richmond Road, No. 157
Richmond Road HE

Thursday 10 October
Andrews Road, Chair Factory AA
Buckingham Road, No. 92 NB
Church Crescent, Lauriston Road HE
Clapton Way, Nos. 105/7 HE
Evering Road HE
Farleigh Road HE
Farleigh Road HE
Kenninghall Road & Maury Road HE

Lower Clapton Road, Nos. 209/11 HE
Millfields Allotments HE
North Milifields Trenches HE
Hillman Street HE
Thistlewaite Road, Nos. 35/39 HE
Victoria Park, Shore Road & St Agnes Terrace UXB
Waterden Road (near) HE

Friday 11 October
Evering Road, No. 85 HE
Maury Road, Nos. 7/17 HE

Saturday 12 October
Brooke Road HE
Cazenove Road, No. 85 HE
Chatsworth Road, junction Lea Bridge Road HE
Duriston Road, No. 32 HE
Evering Road HE
Eastway, Wick Bridge HE
Knightland Road, No. 41 HE
Kyverdale Road, No. 45 NB
Mount Pleasant Lane HE
Northwold Road Estate
Osbaldeston Road, No. 17 HE
Upper Clapton. Road, No. 25 HE
Warwick Court HE

Sunday 13 October
Ardleigh Road, Nos. 1/27 & 2/14 HE
Barnabas Road, junction Wick Road HE
Bergholt Crescent HE
Buckingham Road, Nos. 24/26 HE
Bohemia Place HE
Colveston Crescent, junction Ridley Road AA
Coronation Buildings HE/I
Cow Bridge, Hackney Marshes DA
Dalston Lane, No. 69 HE
Devon Arms, Morning Lane HE
Durley Road, No. 37 HE
Durley Road, No. 66 HE
Eastway, British Industrial Gases DA
Eastway, Eton Manor Ground DA
Englefield Road, rear of No. 51 HE
Eleanor Road, No. 83 UXB
Fox's Lane, Trelawney Road & Morning Lane HE
French Hospital, Victoria Park Road HE
Graham Road, No. 14 I
Graham Road, No. 140 HE
Hackney Station, Miller's Coal Yard HE
Holly Street HE
Holly Street, No. 52 HE
King Edward's Road HE
Lamb Lane, Sidworth Street HE
Lee Conservancy Road DA
Lenthal Road
Lenthal Road, Nos. 15/17 I
Lenthal Road, Nos. 54/56 NB
Lesbia Road BB
London Lane, Railway (Signal) Box HE
Malvern Road
Mapledene Road, No. 75 HE
Mare Street & Well Street HE
Osbaldeston Road, No. 30 UXB
Paragon Road, No. 35 HE
Pemberton Place HE
Penshurst Road HE
Richmond Road HE
Richmond Road, No. 250 HE
Rockmead Road, No. 4 HE
Shore Road, junction Victoria Park Road HE
Tottenham Road HE
Tudor Road, No. 30 HE
Victoria Park, near Royal Gate HE
Wellbury Street OB
Well Street Common HE
West Hackney Church
Wetherall Road HE

Monday 14 October
Berkshire Road, No. 51 HE
Cawley Road HE
Craven Walk, No. 56 HE
Culford Road HE
De Beauvoir Crescent HE
De Beauvoir Square HE
Eastway, Gainborough Road School HE
Englefield Road, No. 53 HE

Englefield Road & Mortimer Road	HE
Englefield Road Baths	OB
Felstead Street & Prince Edward's Road	HE
Hertford Road	AA
Lavender Grove	OB
Leadale Road	HE
Morris's Cabinet Factory	HE
Parkholme Road & Richmond Road	HE/UXB
Southgate Road, No. 132	HE
Tudor Grove	HE
Upton Road	HE

Tuesday 15 October

Adam & Eve, Homerton High Street	HE
Ash Grove, Mare Street	HE
Barnabas Terrace, No. 11	I
Brooksby's Walk, No. 7	OB
Cavendish Mansions	HE
De Beauvoir Road	HE
Fletching Road, No. 68	DA
Forest Road, No. 108	OB
Gayhurst Road Baths	HE
Gayhurst Road, No. 30	HE
Glenarm Road	OB
Glenarm Road	OB
Goulton Road	HE
Holly Street	HE
Homerton High Street	HE
Homerton High Street, Taylor's Buildings	HE
Homerton High Street, No. 126	HE
Labworth's Factory, Tudor Road	HE
Lamb Lane & Sidworth Street	HE
Lansdowne Drive, No. 62	HE
London Fields, path by Martello Street	HE
Mayola Road, Nos. 16/18	DA
Mayola Road, No. 76	HE
Middleton Arms	HE
Millfields Road, No. 128	HE
Powerscroft Road, No. 104	OB
Rectory Road, Nos. 63/5	OB
Richmond Road, Nos. 97/99	OB
Richmond Road, No. 130	HE
Richmond Road, No. 142	HE
Sandringham Road, No. 116	UXB
Shore Road, Carbroke House	HE
Springfield Park, Bowling Green	HE
Stamford Road, outside No. 19	OB
Tudor Road	HE

Wednesday 16 October

Cadogan Terrace Trenches/ London Fields	HE
East Side, Children's Playground	HE
Fox's Lane, Paragon Road, Frampton Park Road	LM
Hackney Downs	UXLM
Hackney Downs Trenches	HE
Hackney Hospital	OB
Lamb Lane Vicarage	OB
Linscott Road	HE
Richmond Road, Goodmans	HE
Stoneham Road & Geldeston Road	HE
Sutton Place, No. 2	OB
Weald Square	NB
Wren's Park House	HE

Thursday 17 October

Ash Grove, Bush's Chemical Factory	UXB
Clapton Common, No. 153	HE
Clapton Common, junction Stamford Hill	HE
Cleveleys Road	HE
De Beauvoir Road, No. 10	HE
Downham Road, No. 72	HE
Evering Road, No. 223	UXAA
Goulton Road, No. 18	HE
Hackney Electricity Works	AA
Hackney Grove	AA
Hackney Marshes, between Hackney Wick Stadium & Factory	UXB
Hackney Wick Stadium	UXB
Rockmead Gate, Victoria Park	AA

Friday 18 October

Abersham Road	HE
St Phillip's Church, Parkholme Road	HE

Rushmore Road, No. 115	UXAA
Sydner Road	
Well Street, No. 53	UXB

Saturday 19 October

Connor Street	HE
Daubeney Road, No. 30	I/HE
Durrington Road, No. 34	OB
Gilda Crescent, No. 9	UXAA
Kingsland Road, between Canal Bridge & Downham	I
Oswald Street & Millfelds Road	HE
Waterden Road Allotments	UXB

Sunday 20 October

Clapton Way, Nos. 93/97	HE
Glicksteins Factory, Waterden Road	
Knightland Road & Warwick Grove	HE
Lansdown Drive, No. 58	DA
Moresby Road	OB
Queensbridge Road School	DA
Waterden Road between Hackney Wick	
Stadium & Carpenters Road	I
Wallis Road	I
Wigan House, No. 96	UXB
Vartry Road, No. 14a	UXAA

Monday 21 October

Brooke Road	HE
De Beauvoir Crescent, No. 77	UXAA
Ellingfort Road, No. 13a	HE
Ickburgh Road	HE
London Fields Trenches	HE
Malvern Road, No. 21	HE
Malvern Road, No. 25	HE
Mapledene Road, No. 152	HE
Martello Street, No. 29	HE
Mount Pleasant Lane	HE/OB
Sach Road	HE/OB
Sherry's Timber Yard	HE
Upper Clapton Road, No. 51	HE
Upper Clapton Road, Nos. 98/100	HE
Upper Clapton Road, No. 102	HE
West Side, London Fields	HE

Wednesday 23 October

Colne Road, No. 17	HE
Overbury Street	HE
Pedro Street	HE
Redwald Road, No. 43	HE

Friday 25 October

Brougham Road	HE
Hackney Marshes, Goat Bridge	UXB
Trederwen Road	HE
Welshpool Street	HE

Sunday 27 October

Kingsland High Street, Dudley's	AA

Monday 28 October

Royal Oak Road & Graham Road	HE

Wednesday 30 October

Southgate Road, No. 110	I
Englefield Road, No. 37	I
Culford Grove, No. 6	I
De Beauvoir Square & Northchurch Road	HE
Englefield Road, between Kingsland Road & De Beauvoir Square	I
Stamford Lodge, forecourt	UXAA

Thursday 31 October

Holly Street	HE
Ridley Road	HE
Sandringham Road	OB

Friday 1 November

Ashwin Street	HE
Darnley Road, Nos. 8/10	HE
Downham Road, No. 84	HE
Gilpin Road	HE
Lea Bridge Green Shelter	HE
Mandeville Street	HE
Mandeville Street, No. 36	HE
Millfields Road	UXB
Northiam Street	HE/OB/I
Reeves Factory, Abbott Street	HE
Ridley Road	HE
Southgate Road & Northchurch Road	HE

Southgate Grove, No. 16	HE
Ufton Road, Nos. 17/18	HE

Saturday 2 November

Bower Road	I
Southgate Grove, No. 12	HE/AA
Victoria Park, St Mark's Church	HE
Ufton Road, No. 25, rear	

Sunday 3 November

Weald Square	UXAA

Tuesday 5 November

Rutland Road	HE

Wednesday 6 November

Balls Pond Road, No. 73	HE
Balls Pond Road, No. 79	HE
Buckingham Road	HE
Evering Road, No. 215	UXAA
Hackney Marshes, Clock Towerfield	UXB
Oldhill Street, No. 12	UXAA
Tottenham Road, Nos. 59/61	HE
Tottenham Square	HE

Thursday 7 November

Amhurst Road, Samuel Lewis Trust Dwellings	HE
Alcester Crescent	HE
April Street	AA
Clapton Way	HE
Downs Park Road, No. 41	HE
Downs Park Road, Nos. 48/50	HE
Hackney Downs, Searchlight	HE
Hackney Marshes, Gun Site	HE
Harrington Hill	HE
Leaside Road	HE
Loweth's Yard, Cecilia Road	HE
Mount Pleasant Lane, Nos. 39/41	HE
Perch Road	HE
Sach Road	HE
St Marks Rise	HE
Sandringham Road	HE
Upper Clapton Road, No. 51	HE
Upper Clapton Road, Nos. 98/100	HE

Friday 8 November

Alconbury Road	HE
Ashwin Street	HE
Brooke Road	HE
Clapton Square	
Colveston Crescent	
Cricketfield Road, No. 77	HE
Congregational Church, Kingsland High Street	HE
Dalston Junction	HE
Downs Road, Nos. 93/5	HE
Dunsmure Road	HE
Durley Road & Denver Road	HE
Evering Road, No. 178	HE
Ferron Road	
Homerton High Street, Taylors Buildings Kingsland Road, between Stanford Road & Dalston Junction	HE
Kingsland Road & Forest Road	HE
Kingsland High Street, No. 70	HE
Kingsland Road, No. 499	HE
Kingsland High Street	
Kenninghall Road, No. 32	HE
Narford Road	HE
Northwold Road	HE
Priestley Street	
Rowhill Mansions	HE
Shacklewell Lade	HE
Vartry Road, Nos. 25/7	HE
Walsingham Road	HE
West Bank, rear, No. 31	HE
West Bank, rear, No. 2	HE
West Bank, rear, No. 12	HE

Sunday 10 November

Amhurst Road, opposite Evelyn Court	HE
Amhurst Road, Lewis Trust Dwellings	HE
Aspland Grove	I
Gore Road & Victoria Park Road	HE
King Edward's Road	HE
Stamford Hill, No. 40	UXB
Victoria Park Road, Nos. 64/6	HE

Monday 11 November

Belfast Road, No. 25	UXB

Cecilia Road, No. 64	I
Gransden Avenue, Nos. 4/6	HE
King Edward's Road, No. 3	HE
Stoke Newington High Street	HE

Tuesday 12 November

Hackney Downs	HE
Samuel Lewis Trust Dwellings	HE
Lower Clapton Road, Post 15	
Shacklewell Lane, No. 104	UXAA

Wednesday 13 November

Graham Road, No. 145	UXAA
Stormont House, Downs Park Road	HE

Thursday 14 November

Pond Lane Bridge	UXAA

Friday 15 November

Amhurst Park, No. 41	HE
Amhurst Park, No. 66	HE
Ardleigh Road, No. 7	UXAA
Dunlace Road	HE
Farleigh Road	UXAA
Glenarm Road, No. 23/7	HE
Northumberland Mansions	HE
Powell House, Lower Clapton Road	HE
Queensdown Road, No. 1	HE
Stamford Hill, No. 153, St Mary's Convent	HE

Saturday 16 November

Alkham Road	LM
Alvington Crescent	I
Annis Road	HE
Ballance Road, Nos. 2/12	HE
Ballance Road & Hassett Road	HE
Barnabas Road & Hassett Road	
Barnabas Road & Wick Road	HE
Beecholme Road, No. 15	HE
Bentham Road, No. 131	HE
Bentham Road	HE
Bentham Road, Rope Ground	HE
Berger Road & Barnabas Road	HE
Berger Road & Marlow Road	
Cecilia Road, No. 104	I
Cricketfield Road, No. 77	HE
Downs Road, No. 107	HE
Hackney Downs	HE
Hackney Marshes	HE
Hackney Marshes, Sherry's Wharf	HE
Homerton Grove	HE
Homerton High Street	HE
Kenninghall Road	I
Lea Bridge Road, No. 35	HE
Lower Clapton Road, Nos. 201/3	HE
Leadale Road	HE
Lower Clapton Road, Nos. 202/10	HE
Marlow Road	
Midhurst Road	I
Marlow Road	HE
Powell Road	HE
Rowhill Mansions	HE
Sedgwick Street	HE
Southwold Road	HE
Victoria Park Road	HE
Victoria Park Road	HE
Victoria Park	HE

Sunday 17 November

Lady Holies School	UXAA

Tuesday 19 November

Wattisfield Road	HE
Downham Road, No. 78	UXAA
Warwick House	UXB

Wednesday 20 November

Cedra Court	HE
Filey Avenue	HE
Gilda Crescent, Nos. 22/24	HE
Latham's Timber Yard	UXB
North Millfields	HE/UXB

Tuesday 26 November

Latham's, Leaside Wharf	HE
Middlesex Wharf, Towpath	HE
Mount Pleasant Hill	HE
Theydon Road, Hunt Partners	UXB

Sunday 8 December

Ballance Road	HE

Bodney Road, Marden House I
Braydon Road, International Chemical Co. I
Cawley Road LM
Cassland Road HE
Dalston Lane & Spurstowe Terrace I
Graham Road, No. 165 I
Harrowgate Road HE/LM
Kyverdale Road, LCC depot I
Kyverdale Road, Nos. 134/138 I
Pembury Road & Amhurst Road I
Portland Avenue, No. 28 HE
Spurstowe Road I

Monday 9 December
Bethune Road & West Bank Railway Embankment HE
Frampton Park Road HE
Glaskin Mews, Portsea Printing Works I
Hackney Downs UXB
Kenninghall Road, No. 64 HE
LNER Railway, Ridley Road HE
Powell Road, No. 50, St James FAP HE
Shore Place I
Tyssen Street, Siemens Factory HE

Thursday 12 December
Mabley Green UXAA

Friday 13 December
Brooke Road, No. 132 UXAA

Saturday 14 December
Harrowgate Road, No. 51 UXAA

Friday 27 December
Frampton Park Road HE
Middleton Road HE
Oldhill Street HE

Sunday 29 December
Amhurst Road, No. 105 I
Clapton Square
Downs Park Road, Grocers School I
Evering Road HE
Hackney Downs HE/I
Hertford Road, No. 124 HE
Hollar Road, No. 8 UXB
Kenton Road, Wardens Post
Loddiges Road I
Mare Street, No. 385 I
Mortimer Road, Englefield Road HE
Railway Embankment, Richmond Road UXB/HE

Monday 30 December
Mortimer Road, No. 105 HE

1941
Wednesday 1 January
Evering Road, No. 19 UXB

Saturday 11 January
East Bank HE
Holmleigh Road, No. 136 HE
Linthorpe Road HE
Pedro Street HE
Prince Edward Road HE

Wednesday 15 January
Downham Road, No. 53 HE
Benyon Road, Nos. 28/30 HE

Tuesday 28 January
Olinda Road, Stamford Hill HE

Friday 14 February
Kingsmead Estate, Hackney Marsh HE

Monday 17 February
Harrowgate Road, No. 14 AA
Windus Road I

Saturday 8 March
Almack Road HE
Laura Place HE
Lower Clapton Road, Nos. 136/140 HE
Middleton Road & Lansdowne Drive I

Sunday 9 March
Ballance Road & Kenworthy Road, RC Church HE

Monday 10 March

Ruckholt Road, end of. 100 yards rear of Barrage Balloon Site UXB

Tuesday 18 March

Lesbia Road HE
Millfields, near Bandstand HE
Glenarm Road, rear of HE

Wednesday 19 March

Ardleigh Road I
Ballance Road
Bentham Road
Brooke Road, No. 165 I
Brooksbank Street HE
Buckingham Road, Nos. 67, 74, 80 & 92 I
Cassland Road, No. 185 HE
Culford Grove I
Danville Road HE
De Beauvoir Dwelling House, Nos. 85/89 I
Elsdale Street HE
Evering Road, Nos. 200/202 I
Felstead Street HE
Frampton Park Road HE
Goulton Road HE
Hillstowe Street HE
Ickburgh Road I
Kingsland Road, No. 409 I
Latham's Timber Yard HE
Leaside Road HE
Leweston Place, No. 24 AA

Wednesday 19 March

Lower Clapton Road, premises to the rear of Rink Cinema HE
Lower Clapton Road, rear No. 30 UXAA
Mare Street LM/HE
Median Road, Nos. 26 & 28 HE
Middlesex Wharf HE
Morning Lane HE
Mortimer Road, No. 91 I
Queensbridge Road, No. 369 HE
Raynor Street HE
Rock Road HE
Rectory Road, No. 75 HE
Southgate Road, Nos. 172 & 190 I
Southwold Road I
Theydon Road, Hunt Partners I
Theydon Road, Shurmurs I
Wansbeck Road LM
Wick Road I

Friday 21 March

Hackney Church Yard UXB/UXAA

Tuesday 15 April

Rossington Street AA

Wednesday 16 April

Stamford Hill UXAA

Thursday 17 April

Arbutus Street LM
Casterton Street LM
Coles Road LM
Halidon Street, No. 32a UXAA
Rushmore Road, Nos. 48/50 UXAA

Saturday 19 April

Annis Road, Nos. 32/36 HE
Ballance Road HE
Cadogan Terrace DA
Danesdale Road
Egerton Road LM
Hackney Marshes LM
Latham's Timber Yard HE/I
Oriel Road HE
Waterden Road UXLM

Saturday 10 May

This file is missing although the following areas are recorded as being hit:

Andrews Road, Nos. 41 & 54
Ashtead Road, Nos. 37/41
Balmes Road, No. 6
Cawley Road
Chatsworth Road
Chatsworth Road
Chatsworth Road, Tennis Courts

Chailey Street
Christie Road
Cricketfield Road
De Beauvoir Square
Freemont Street
Gascoyne Road
Holt's Timber Yard
Jackman Street
King Edward Road
King Edward Road, Nos. 81/91
Laurel Street, No. 16
Lauriston Road
Lower Clapton Road, No. 179
Mildenhall Road
Mildenhall Road, No. 84
North Millfields Allotments
Richmond Road
Shore Road
Sheep Lane, No. 68
St Marks Rise
Ufton Road
Victoria Park Road
Victoria Park (Cottage)
Wattisfield Road
Wick Road

Monday 28 July
Cassland Road HE
Dunsmure Road, Nos. 24 & 26 AA
Morpeth Road HE

1942
Wednesday 3 June
Penshurst Road I

Wednesday 10 June
Bramshaw Road UXB

Tuesday 28 July
Gilpin Road NB
Waterden Road, Oxo Factory AA

Friday 31 July
Alvington Crescent, No. 52 (Shacklewell Lane) AA
De Beauvoir Crescent HE

1943
Sunday 17 January
Loddiges Road, No. 4 AA

Wednesday 3 March
Dalston Lane, No. 235 AA

Wednesday 19 May
Gunton Road, Nos. 65/67/69/71 HE
Southwold Road HE

1944
Friday 21 January
Casterton Street AA

Saturday 29 January
Retreat Place, between Meads Place & Morning Lane PM

Friday 4 February
Lea Bridge Road, 2A, Casimir & Fletching Roads I
Dalston Lane, No. 39 AA

Saturday 19 February
Balls Pond Road, outside No. 15 AA
Warwick Grove, between Mt Pleasant Lane & Moresby Road HE
Glenarm Road, between Chatsworth Road/Median Road HE
Blurton Road, between Chatsworth Road/Elderfield Road HE
Clapton Common, No. 109 HE
Southwold, Gunton, Cleveleys & Detmold Roads, Warwick Grove, Alcester Crescent, Clapton Station I
Comberton Road, between Mt Pleasant Lane & Southwold Road I
Millfields Road, Allotment 149 HE
Powerscroft Road, No. 123 AA
Inightland Road, No. 18 UXB
Tow Path, Hackney Marsh Side

Sunday 20 February
Lenthall road, Nos. 42/44 AA

Wednesday 23 February
Nightingale Road, outside No. 74 AA
Lawley Street, No. 7 AA
Foulden Road, No. 71 AA
Springfield Park, Springhill UXAA
Clapton Signal Box, Clapton Junction UXAA

Thursday 24 February
Evelyn Court/Amhurst Road Shelter I
Downham Road, No. 121 AA

Wednesday 22 March
Kingsmead Estate/Ironside House, No. 37 AA
Wick Road, No. 426 AA

Tuesday 13 June
Victoria Park Road, No. 202 RS

Friday 16 June
Clapton Way, No. 48 AA

Saturday 17 June
Elrington Road, No. 15 AA
London Fields, West Side, Shelter 226 V1

Sunday 18 June
Rushmore and Chatsworth Roads V1
Stoke Newington Road/ Kingsland High Street HE
Danesdale Road/Victoria Park Road V1

Thursday 22 June
Riverside Works, Leaside Road, Shurmur's Victory Works V1

Tuesday 27 June
Mount Pleasant Lane, Warwick Grove

Wednesday 28 June
Cleveleys, Gunton and Casimir Roads

Saturday 1 July
Overbury Street V1

Monday 3 July
Rectory Road, between Farleigh & Foulden Roads V1

Wednesday 5 July
Morpeth Road/Gore Road V1

Friday 7 July
Richmond Road, between Lansdowne Greenwood Roads V1

Saturday 8 July
Cowdray Street, junction of Kenworthy Road V1

Sunday 9 July
Junction of Heatherley Place & Benthal Road V1

Wednesday 12 July
Eastway, between Osborne Road & Daintry Street V1

Sunday 16 July
Meeson Street, between Daubeney Road Adley Street V1

Tuesday 18 July
Bethune Road, Stoke Newington side, Dunsmure Road V1

Wednesday 19 July
Braydon Road & Firsby Road
Darenth Road, between Portland Avenue & Lymouth Road V1
Moundfield Road, between Craven Park Road & Ravensdale Road V1

Sunday 23 July
Birchington House, Pembury Estate, Pembury Road V1
Amhurst Road; corner Marcon Place V1
Wood Dump, Hackney Marshes V1

Thursday 27 July
Eastway, opposite Mission Church V1

Saturday 29 July
Northwold Road, Upper Clapton Road V1
Triangle, Mare Street V1
Haggerston Road, Mayfield Road V1

Sunday 30 July
Cawley Road, Victoria Park Road V1
Greenwood Road /Forest Road/ Richmond Road V1

Monday 31 July
Gun Site, Canal Bank, Hackney Marshes V1

Wednesday 2 August
Berkshire Road, outside Fire Station V1

Thursday 3 August
Rockmead Road, facing Victoria Park V1

Tuesday 8 August
St Barnabas Church, Homerton V1

Sunday 13 August
Millfields Road, junction Chailey Street V1

Tuesday.15 August
Gun Site, Hackney Marshes V1

Thursday 17 August
Narford Road V1

Thursday 24 August
Rendlesha u Road & Maury Road V1

Wednesday 30 August
Temple Mills Road, allotments at back of White Hart Hotel V1

Saturday 21 October
Prout Road/Beecholme Road V1

Thursday 26 October
Radley's Boathouse, Springhill V2/GB

Sunday 19 November
Chatham Place, between Morning Lane & Paragon Road V2

Thursday 7 December
Cawley, Wetherell and Rockmead Roads V2

Saturday 23 December
Shore Place V2

1945
Thursday 4 January
Woodland Street, between Forest & Richmond Roads V2

Monday 15 January
Hackney Downs, north of Bandstand, opp. Oakfield Road V2

Thursday 1 February
Windus Road, between Lampard Grove & Cazenove Road

Sunday 4 February
Adley Street, junction of Marsh Hill V2

Monday 5 February
Exmouth Place V2

Monday 12 February
Mabley Street, crater in Mabley Green

Stoke Newington

1940
Sunday 8 September
Junction Green Lane & Church Street I
Clissold Crescent, between Albion & Winston Roads I
Opp. Abney Park Cemetery &

Infants School I
Palatine Road, No. 64 I
Dynevor Road, Nos. 85–87, between Chesham & Lavers I
Lavers Road, junction Dynevor Road HE
Clissold Road, rear of garden I
Dynevor Road, near High Street HE
St Annes Road, centre Seven Sisters I
Lordship Road, No. 120 I
Green Lanes, No. 138 I
Lordship Road, No. 128 I
Seven Sisters, No. 285 I
Clissold Park I
Lordship Park, No. 50 I
Lordship Road, No. 140 I
Woodberry Down, No. 8 I
Eade Road, No. 12 I
Green Lanes, No. 46 I
Paget Road & St Andrews Manor Road, Railway Goods Siding I
Manor Road, garden, No. 76 I
Princess May Road, school HE
Abney Park Cemetery I
Lordship Road, rear of No. 102 I
Bouverie Road, No. 56 I
Palatine Road, No. 3 I
Spencer Grove, No. 97 I
Brighton Road, No. 15, Leonards Place I
Allen Road I
Allen Road, No. 14 I
Corner of Beatty Road, No. 20 I
Albion Road I
Neville Road, No. 25 I
Allen Road, No. 103 I
Junction Kersley Road & Church Street UXB
Lordship Park, No. 39 HE
Clissold Park, opp. Clissold Court I
Walford Road, No. 68, near Brighton Road HE
Lancell Street, No. 13 UXB
Brighton Road, No. 63 HE
Palatine Road, Nos. 40–54 HE
Lordship Park, rear of No. 34, & Grazebrook Road HE

Monday 9 September
Wordsworth Road school HE
Gunstor Road, No. 2 UXB
Green Lanes, No. 317 UXB
Queens Drive, No. 104 HE
Queens Drive, Nos. 112–118 HE
Digby Crescent, No. 49 I
Queens Drive, No. 126 I
Seven Sisters Road, No. 410 UXB
Woodberry Grove, No. 25 UXB
Hayling Road, No. 26 I
Matthias Road School I
S.N. Church Street, rear of Town Hall UXB
Woodberry Grove, No. 2 UXAA
Lordship Park, Nos. 28–30 UXB

Tuesday 10 September
Wilberforce Road, No. 8 I
Clissold Crescent, between Albion & Springdale Roads HE

Wednesday 11 September
Harcombe & Sandbrook Roads HE
Carysfort Road, No. 10 HE
Junction Kynaston Road & Defoe Road HE
Ayrsome Road, Oldfield Road & Marton Road HE

Thursday 12 September
Neville Road, No. 118 AA

Saturday 14 September
Green Lanes, rear of No. 92 HE
South Bank East Reservoir UXAA

Sunday 15 September
Burma Mews, Church Passage HE

Monday 16 September
Junction Albion Road UXAA
Manor Road I
Junction Manor Road & Lordship Road I
Grayling Road, No. 16 I
Green Lanes, No. 165 I

Green Lanes & Church Street I
Fairholt Road, No. 17 I
Church Walk I
Cheshoim Road I
Beatty Road I
Yorkshire Grove I
Victorian Grove, Pyjama Factory I
High Street, opp. Brook Road I
S.N. Church Street, corner Summerhouse Road I
Seven Sisters Road, near Manor House & Portland Rise I
Manor House area I
Heathland Road, No. 28 HE
Densmore Road, No. 93 I
Beaulieu Villas, Seven Sisters Road I
Woodberry Grove, No. 25 UXB
St Kildas & St Andrews Roads I
Chesholm Road, No. 46 I
Manor Road, No. 121 I
Lordship Road, No. 117 I
Junction Gunster Road & Walford Road I
Beatty Road, outside No. 36 I

Tuesday 17 September

High Street, rear of White Hart Hotel I
Coronation Avenue I
Londesborough Road, No. 40 I
Green Lanes, No. 295 I
Richards Shelter I
Junction Amhurst Park & Seven Sisters Road HE
Oldfield Road, No. 45 I
Barbauld Road, No. 50 I
Lordship Park, No. 94 I
Pellerin Road, No. 46 I
Fairholt Road, No. 96 UXB
Woodberry Down, No. 34 HE
S.N. Church Street School I
Lordship Park I
S.N. Church St Depot I
Carysfort Road, No. 97 I
S.N. Church Street, Rose & Crown, pub I
Greenway Close I
Green Lanes, No. 273 I
Carysfort Road, No. 37 I
Lordship Terrace, Denman House I
Spencer Works, No. 22a Bouverie Road I
Harcombe Road, junction Sandbrook Road I
Shelford Place, S.N. Church Street I
Newington Green, opp. Mildmay Hospital I
Carysfort Road, Nos. 34–38 I

Wednesday 18 September

Abney Hall, S.N. Church Street I
Clissold FAP I
Matthias Road, No. 100 UXAA
32 Yoakley Road I
Sketchley Dye Works, Bouverie Road I
Lordship Road, Nos. 46–58 I
Lordship Park, No. 42 I
Green Lanes, No. 213 I
S.N. Church Street, No. 116 I
Listria Park, No. 1 HE
S.N. High Street, by Victorian Road HE
Bouverie Road UXB
Lordship Road, No. 178 UXAA
Lordship Road, No. 64 UXAA
Manor Road, No. 49 HE
S.N. High Street, Dynevor Road HE
Manor Road, No. 77, Convent HE
Stamford Hill, No. 27 HE

Thursday 19 September

Junction Seven Sisters & Woodberry Grove I
Lordship Road, No. 210 I
Blackstock Road, No. 159 I
Digby Crescent, No. 2 I
Kings Crescent, No. 13 I
Warwick House, No. 257 S.N. Church Street HE
Queens Drive, No. 69 I
Guttesby, Nos. 113–115 S.N. High Street HE
Green Lanes Transport Office & Brownswood, Lordship & Manor Roads I
Finsbury Park Road, No. 31 I

Lordship Road, No. 89 I
Wilberforce Road, No. 95 I
Queens Drive, No. 80 I
Finsbury Park Road, No. 67 I
Green Lanes, No. 208 AA
Wilberforce Road, No. 88 I
S.N. Church Street, No. 137 AA
Kings Crescent, No. 23 I
Denham House, S.N. Church Street I
LCC Housing Estate, S.N. Church Street I
Clissold Road, No. 9 I

Friday 20 September
St Andrews Grove, No. 31 UXAA
Allerton Road, No. 10 UXAA
Bruce Lodge, Green Lanes HE
Palatine Road, No. 24 HE

Saturday 21 September
Allerton Road, No. 10 HE
S.N. Church Street, opp. No. 4 AA
Bethune Road, No. 93 UXAA
Digby Crescent, No. 35 I
Kings Crescent, No. 4 I
Bethune Road, No. 94 I
Brownswood Road, No. 54 I

Sunday 22 September
Green Lanes, No. 231 I
Digby Crescent, No. 71 I
Queens Drive, No. 118 I
St Kildas Road, No. 51 I
Finsbury Park Road, No. 103 I
Blackstock Road, No. 151 I
Green Lanes, No. 216 I
Queens Drive, No. 69 I
Lordship Road, No. 117 I
Brownswood Road, No. 56 I
Lordship Road, No. 198 I
Lordship Road, No. 188 I
Brownswood Tavern, Green Lanes I
Eade Road, Courtney Popes Work UXAA
Manor Road area HE

Monday 23 September
Green Lanes, No. 313 UXAA
Bethune Road, No. 99 HE

Tuesday 24 September
Junction Clonbrook & Neville Roads HE
Neville Road, No. 16e HE
Neville Road, No. 93 HE
Harcombe Road, No. 49 HE
Albion Road, No. 216 UXB
Clissold Park HE
Dumont Road, No. 6 HE
Fairholt Road, Rhodes Garage HE
Church Walk, Strouds Nursery HE
Milton Grove, No. 53 AA
Clissold Road, opp. LCC Flats UXB
Spencer Grove, No. 12 AA
Dynevor Road, No. 85 UXM

Wednesday 25 September
Shellgrove Road, No. 13 I

Thursday 26 September
Blackstock Road, No. 157 I
Between Collins Road & Green Lanes I
Clissold Park I
Carysfort Road I

Friday 27 September
Winston Road, No. 2 HE
Clissold Crescent, No. 34 I
Clissold Crescent, No. 129 I
Clissold Park Area I
Blackstock Road, No. 87 I
Winston Road, No. 148, & Millington House I
Queens Drive, No. 131 UXAA
St Matthias Church I
Carysfort Road, Nos. 38/56, corner Albion Road I
S. Newington Road, No. 71 I
Cressington Road, Woolfs Factory I
Clissold Crescent, No. 93 I
Derwent House, between Howard & Matthias Roads I
Devonshire Sq. Church, S.N. Road I

Winston Road, No. 161	I
Winston Road, No. 118	I
Albion Road, No. 99	I
Cressington Road, No. 9	I
Lavell Street, No. 4	I
Winston Road, Nos. 74, 81, 94, 107	I

Saturday 28 September

Barretts Grove, No. 42	HE

Monday 30 September

Green Lanes, No. 223	HE
Clissold Crescent, Nos. 125/127	HE
Clissold Park, between Church Street & Lordship Road	HE

Thursday 3 October

Londesborough Road, No. 52, between Barbauld & Clonbrook Roads	HE
E. Reservoir South Bank, near Watermans Cottages	UXB
Albion Road, Nos. 181/183	HE
Queen Elizabeth Walk, No. 92	HE
Seven Sisters Road, No. 472	UXB
Lordship Road, No. 67	HE
Old St Marys Church Yard	HE

Friday 4 October

Spencer Grove, No. 57	HE

Saturday 5 October

Shakespeare Walk, No. 115	UXAA
Portland Rise, near Seven Sisters	OB
Bethune Road, No. 28	I
Heathland Road, No. 23	I

Sunday 6 October

Portland Rise, No. 7	OB

Tuesday 8 October

Finsbury Park Road, Nos. 76 & 78	OB
Pellerin Road, No. 10	UXAA
Lordship Road, Nos. 142/4	OB

Wednesday 9 October

Finsbury Park Road, No. 103	AA
Green Lanes, No. 188	HE
Queen Elizabeth Walk, No. 1	HE
Grazebrook Road, No. 2	HE
Milton Grove	HE
White Hart, No. 33 S.N. High Street	I
Victorian Grove, Factory	I
Prince George Road, No. 54	I
S.N. Church Street, No. 46	I
Defoe Road, No. 25	I
Dynevor Road, No. 11	I
Dynevor Road, No. 119	I
Church Walk, near LCC School	OB

Thursday 10 October

Manor House Hotel	HE
Green Lanes, No. 380	I
Millard Road, Nos. 26/28	HE
Boleyn Road, Filter Beds	HE

Friday 11 October

Green Lanes	UXB
Eade Road, No. 6	HE
Queens Drive, Nos. 123/125	HE

Saturday 12 October

Manor Road, Convent	HE

Sunday 13 October

Albion Road, No. 206	HE
Sandbrook Road, No. 12	HE
Kingsway, Nos. 2/4 (Albion Road)	HE
Palatine Road, Nos. 46/48	HE
Brighton Road, Nos. 70/74	HE
Watford Road, Nos. 84/86	HE
Knebworth Road, Nos. 6/7	HE
Neville Road, No. 41	HE
Cowper Road, No. 93	HE
Old & New St Marys Churches S.N. Church Street	HE
Albion Road, No. 51, Wheelers Factory	HE
Albion Road, No. 184	HE
Barbould Road, No. 44	UXB
S. Newington Road, Nos. 157/161, No. 5 Shelter	HE
Cowper Road, No. 80	UXB

Albion Road, No. 186 HE
Albion Road, No. 217 HE
Clissold Park, Playground HE
Old St Marys Church, Clissold Park HE
Londesborough Road, No. 49 HE
Clissold Park, Tennis Court, Springdale Road UXB

Monday 14 October
Junction Green Lanes HE
Mãnon Fréres, Springdale Road HE
Green Lanes, No. 138 OB

Tuesday 15 October
Times Fur Co., Seven Sisters Road I
Drill Hall, Albion Road HE

Wednesday 16 October
Belgrade Road, No. 34 HE
Gunstor Road, No. 12 HE
Barbauld Road, No. 33 HE
Corner of Harcombe & Barbould Road HE
Sandbrook Road, Nos. 35/37 HE
Prince George Road, No. 32 HE
Brighton Road, No. 82 HE
Brighton Road, No. 69 HE
Palatine Road, No. 48 HE
Palatine Road, Nos. 39/41 HE

Saturday 19 October
Abney Park Cemetery AA
Prince George Road HE
Lordship Road, No. 101 OB
Lordship Park, No. 42 OB
Clissold Park, near Bridge HE
Clissold Park, neax Boating Lake HE
Clissold Park HE
Abney Park, rear of High Street HE

Tuesday 29 October
Shakespeare Walk, No. 30 UXAA
Dumont Road, No. 17 UXAA

Thursday 31 October
Princess May Road school HE
Clissold Crescent, No. 67 UXAA

Friday 1 November
Knebworth Road & vicinity I
near Milton Depot I
Burma Road, rear of No. 40 I
Prince George Road & Wordsworth Road Cl Area I
Neville Road, No. 85 I
Wordsworth Road School I
between Barbould Road & Albion Road I
Clissold Road, No. 1 I
Clissold Crescent, No. 5 I
Lordship Park Mews, No. 2 AA

Wednesday 6 November
Watson Street, Nos. 37/39 HE
Matthias Road, Nos. 85/87 HE
Hewling Flats, Matthias Road HE
Watson Street, Nos. 25/27 HE

Thursday 7 November
Albion Road, Nos. 48/50 HE

Friday 8 November
Bouverie Road, No. 52 UXAA
Manor Road, No. 93 HE
Grange Court Road & Heathland Road HE
Bethune Road, No. 51 HE

Saturday 9 November
Heathland Road, No. 6 HE
Grayling Road, No. 23 HE

Sunday 10 November
Wilberforce Road, Nos. 91/93 UXB
Gloucester Drive, Nos. 66/70 HE
Filter Beds, Green Lanes, Nos. 4/5 HE
Green Lanes, No. 215 HE

Monday 11 November
Green Lanes, No. 202 UXB
Yoakley Road, No. 31 UXB
Bouverie Road, No. 62 UXB

Lordship Road, No. 55	UXB
Yoakley Road, No. 100	UXB
Manor Road, No. 4	UXB
Digby Crescent, No. 65	UXB
Digby Crescent, No. 35	UXB
Junction Queens Drive & Digby Crescent	I
Digby Crescent, No. 79	UXB
Finsbury Park Road, No. 41	UXB
Finsbury Park Road, No. 31	UXB
S.N. High Street, junction High Street & Victorian Grove	HE
Neville Road, No. 19	HE
Milton Grove, No. 10	HE
Shakespeare Walk, Nos. 22/24	HE
Junction Gunstor & Walford Roads	HE
Walford Road, Nos. 87/91	HE
Shipway Terrace, No. 142	HE
Allen Road, No. 8	HE
Spencer Grove, No. 80	HE
Orpen Road, No. 2a	HE
Spencer Grove, Nos. 95/99	HE
Victorian Road, No. 13	HE
Mildmay Club grounds	HE
Listria Park, No. 33	UXB
Watson Street, No. 13	HE
Lordship Road, No. 106	UXB
Shakespeare Walk, No. 12	HE
Abney Park Cemetery	UXB
Martaban Road, No. 23	UXB
Wilberforce Road, No. 67	UXB
Queens Drive, No. 86	UXB
No. 9 Filter Bed MWB	UXB
Lordship Park, No. 20	UXB
Digby Crescent, No. 55	UXB
Brownswood Road, No. 27	I
Queens Drive, No. 113	UXB
Lordship Park, No. 12	UXB

Tuesday 12 November

Queens Drive, No. 88	UXB

Friday 15 November

Clissold Park	HE
Bethune Road, No. 83	UXB
Manor House near Finsbury Park, Green Lanes	HE
Green Lanes, No. 266	HE
Junction Woodberry Grove, Green Lanes Manor House, end	HE

Saturday 16 November

Lordship Park, No. 54	HE
Bruce Lodge, Green Lanes	HE
Albion Road, No. 200a	M

Sunday 17 November

Yoakley Road, No. 82	UXB

Thursday 28 November

Palatine Road, No. 84	UXAA

Sunday 29 December

Abney Park Cemetery	HE
Manor House	MOL
Abney Park Cemetery	HE

1941

Sunday 5 January

St Matthias Square	M
St Matthias Church Ground	M

Saturday 11 January

Seven Sisters Road, No. 298	I
St Johns Church, Gloucester Drive	I
Manor Road, No. 69	HE
Corner of Leconfield Road & Peterton Road	HE
Clissold Park	I
Finsbury Park Road, No. 9	I
Area Alex. Court, Seven Sisters Road, No. 330	I
Finsbury Park Road, Garage adjoining No. 11	I
Abney Park Cemetery	HE

Wednesday 26 February

Portland Rise & Green Lanes	HE
Londesborough Road, No. 13	UXAA

Wednesday 19 March

Bethune Road, No. 137	HE

Wednesday 16 April

St Johns Church, Gloucester Drive	I
Princess Crescent, No. 3	I
Queens Drive, No. 84 or 86	I
Queens Drive & Kings Crescent	AA
Queens Drive, No. 109	I
Wilberforce Road, No. 70	I
Wilberforce Road, No. 101	I
Seven Sisters Road, No. 332	I

Thursday 17 April

Digby Crescent, No. 28	I
Clissold Park Animal Enclosure	M
Clissold Park, near Grazebrook, & Queen Elizabeth Walk Gate	UXM
Gloucester Drive, No. 8	I
St Johns Church Vicarage	I
Princess Crescent, No. 18	I
Queens Drive, No. 122	I
Queens Drive, No. 76	I
Wilberforce Road, No. 90	I
Gloucester Drive, No. 4	I
Finsbury Park Road, No. 79	I
Finsbury Park Road, No. 101	I
Wilberforce Road, No. 79	I
Gloucester Drive, No. 33	I
Princess Crescent, No. 8	I
Gloucester Drive, No. 11	I
Wilberforce Road, No. 37	I
Wilberforce Road, No. 50	I
Wilberforce Road, No. 60	I
Wilberforce Road, No. 67	I
Queens Drive, No. 132	I
Blackstock Road, No. 95	I
Blackstock Road, No. 121	I
Blackstock Road, No. 143	I
Blackstock Road, No. 143a	I
Blackstock Road, No. 175	I
Queens Drive, No. 96	I
Queens Drive, No. 128	I
Queens Drive, No. 151	I
Queens Drive, No. 104	I
Finsbury Park Road, No. 92	I
Finsbury Park Road, No. 80	I
Wilberforce Road, No. 32	I
Finsbury Park Road, No. 99	I
Seven Sisters Road, No. 334	I
Adolphus Road, No. 11	I
Adolphus Road, No. 21	I
Henry Road, No. 10	I
Dropped in gardens & roads	I
Somerfield Road, No. 2	I

Saturday 19 April

Ship Press, Green Lanes	HE
Green Lanes, No. 268	HE
Milton Grove, Albion Road end	AA
Seven Sisters Road, Nos. 414/416	HE
Abney Park Cemetery	M
Bouverie Road, rear of No. 44	UXM
Woodberry Down, Nos. 10/12	HE

1943

Sunday 17 January

Allerton Road, No. 42	AA

Monday 18 Janaury

Portland Rise, No. 33	UXAA

Wednesday 3 March

Listria Park, No. 77	AA
Green Lanes, No. 2	AA
Lordship Road, No. 142	UXAA

Monday 18 October

Shellgrove Road, No. 15	AA
Grayling Road, No. 11	UXAA

Thursday 7 October

Yoakley Road, No. 32a	AA

1944

Saturday 29 January

Green Lanes, No. 250	I
Green Lanes, No. 259	I
Springdale Road, No. 69	UXAA
Green Lanes, junction Church Street	AA
St Midas Road, outside No. 49	I
Heathland Road, roadway	I

Saturday 19 February
Lidfield Road, No. 22 HE
Lidfield Road, No. 31 HE
Albion Road, No. 71 HE
Albion Road, No. 72 HE
Milton Grove, No. 85 HE
Shakespeare Walk, No. 126 HE
Nevill Road, No. 120 HE
Eade Road, No. 17 HE
Blackstock Road, No. 9 UXAA

Wednesday 23 February
Amhurst Park, No. 98 AA

Tuesday 14 March
Water Works, Green Lanes AA
Fairholt Road, No. 98 UXAA
Green Lanes, No. 268 UXAA

Wednesday 22 March
Manor Road, Nos. 3/11 AA
Princess Crescent, No. 3 UXAA
Lordship Road, No. 158 UXAA

Wednesday 19 April
Harcombe Road, No. 54 UXAA

Thursday 20 April
Green Lanes, No. 243 UXAA

Wednesday 17 May
Albion Road, No. 176 UXAA

Thursday 15 June
Alexandra Grove, No. 27 UXAA

Sunday 18 June
Knebworth Road, Londesborough & Nevill Roads V1

Sunday 25 June
Defoe Road V1
Finsbury Park (boundary incident) V1

Sunday 2 July
Petherton Road (boundary incident) V1

Tuesday 4 July
Finsbury Park (boundary incident) V1

Sunday 9 July
Woodberry Down, No. 31 V1

Tuesday 18 July
Bethune Road, No. 68 V1

Friday 28 July
Woodberry Down, No. 42 V1

Wednesday 23 August
Clissold Crescent V1

Tuesday 29 August
Cyprus Laundry, Hermitage Road V1

Thursday 16 November
Mayville Road (boundary incident) V2

1945
Monday 8 January
Green Lanes, between Lordship Park & Portland Rise V2

Wednesday 10 January
Green Lanes, rear of No. 252 V2

Sunday 14 January
Finsbury Park, opp. Finsbury Park Road (boundary incident) V1

Hoxton and the Pitfield Street Area of Shoreditch

1940
Sunday 25 August
Bacchus Walk UXB
Kingsland railway bridge UXB

Thursday 29 August
Academy Buildings, Fanshaw Street HE

Sunday 8 September
Pitfield Street, No. 228 — Not recorded

Monday 9 September
Pitfield Street, No: 252 — HE

Wednesday 11 September
Pitfield Street, No. 268 — UXB
Kingsland Road, No. 247 — UXB
Wilkes Place — I
Pitfield Street, near school — I
Crondall Street — UXB

Friday 13 September
Hoxton Street, rear No. 111 — UXB
Kingsland Road, No. 176 — I

Saturday 14 September
Cremer Street railway bridge — I
Kingsland Road, No. 247 — UXB

Sunday 15 September
Shenfield Street, No. 36 (?) — UXAA

Wednesday 18 September
Crondall Street — I
Crondall Street School — I
Cherbury Street — I

Thursday 19 September
Bookham Street — I
Pitfield Street, No. 126 (?) rear — I

Tuesday 8 October
Bevenden Yard — I
Freeman's Tobacco Company, Pitfield Street, Hoxton Street — I
Bacchus Walk — HE
Hoxton Street, junction with Old Street — HE
Myrtle Street — HE
Hoxton Square — HE
Kingsland Road, rear No. 262 — HE
Purcell Street — I
Pitfield Street, rear No. 119 — I
Turners Square — I
St Leonards Dwellings — I
Crondall Street, junction with New North Road — I

Wednesday 9 October
Bevenden Street — HE
Pitfield Street/Haberdasher Street junction — I
Crondall Street — I
Pitfield Street/New North Road — I
St Monica's Church, Hoxton Square — I
Crondall Street — I
Bookham Street/Cherbury Street — I
Pitfield Street School and House — I
Bright Mews, Hoxton Street — I
Russells Timber Yard, Bevenden Street — I
Hoxton Square — HE

Thursday 10 October
Hoxton Street, No. 175 — I

Sunday 13 October
Fanshaw Street/Hoxton Street junction — HE
Hoxton Hall School — UXB
Caroline Place — HE

Monday 14 October
Myrtle Street, junction Hoxton Street — HE
Redvers Street — HE
Shenfield Street and Falkirk Street — HE
Kingsland Road, No. 78 — HE

Tuesday 15 October
Geffrye Museum, Kingsland Road — HE
Hoxton Square — HE
ARP Club, New North Road — HE
Crondall Street between Pitfield Street and New North Road — I
Recreation Ground between Aske Street and Fanshaw Street — HE

Wednesday 16 October
Leasks Stores, Hoxton Street I

Friday 25 October
Drysdale Street I
Falkirk Street I
Bacchus Walk I
Homefield Street I
Bevenden Street, Dotteridges (undertakers) I
Wilkes Place I
Pitfield Street, St Johns Place I
New North Road, No. 23 I

Saturday 26 October
Hoxton Street, junction with Redvers Street and Britannia Theatre HR&I
Pitfield Street and Crondall Street junction I
Kingsland Road, No. 228 HE

Saturday 9 November
Technical Institute UXB

Sunday 8 December
Bevenden Street HE
Aske House, Fanshaw Street HE
Basing House Yard HE
Myrtle Street HE
Aske Street HE
Buckland Street HE
Basing House Yard HE

Sunday 28 December
Drysdale Street HE

1941
Saturday 8 March
Fleming Street HE
Basing Place HE

Sunday 20 April
Technical Institute, Pitfield Street M

Saturday 10 May
Hoxton Baths I
Hoxton Street HE
Aske House, Fanshaw Street HE
Royal Oak public house and area between Ashford Street and Pitfield Street HE
Hoxton Street, No. 77 and Oxleys I
Hoxton Square, Brands I
Crondall Street HE
Purcell Street HE
Bacchus Walk HE

1944
Friday 21 January
Technical Institute AA

Sunday 6 August
Caroline Gardens V1

Index

Printed in Great Britain
by Amazon